EMU After Maastricht

Peter B. Kenen

Published by
Group of Thirty©
Washington, DC
1992

Table of Contents

I. Introduction

On December 10, 1991, at the Maastricht Summit, the member states of the European Community (EC) adopted comprehensive amendments to the 1957 Treaty of Rome. When ratified by all the EC countries, the amendments will extend the domain of the Community in many directions. This monograph deals with the group of amendments concerned with Economic and Monetary Union (EMU). They provide for the establishment of a European System of Central Banks (ESCB), with a European Central Bank (ECB) at its center, and for the creation of a single currency, the ECU, to replace the currencies of the EC countries.[1]

Much has written about this subject, and much more will be written in the years ahead. This monograph will not cover all of the issues raised in that vast literature or dwell on the many opportunities and options rejected or ignored on the way to Maastricht. It will focus on the plan adopted at Maastricht, its implications for the form and functioning of EMU, the problems of transition, and the likely consequences of the plan for the international monetary system.

This first chapter looks back at the origins of EMU and the events that led to the Maastricht Agreement. The next chapter describes the organization and mandate of the new central-banking system. The third chapter looks

---

[1] These matters are covered in Title VI of the Treaty, the Statute of the European System of Central Banks and of the European Central Bank (cited here as the ESCB Statute), the Statute of the European Monetary Institute (cited here as the EMI Statute), and certain protocols attached to the Treaty. Two other documents are cited here: The draft of the ESCB Statute prepared by the Committee of Central Bank Governors and dated November 27, 1990 (cited as the Governors Draft), and the drafts of the Treaty, ESCB Statute, and EMI Statute prepared by the Netherlands Presidency and dated October 28, 1991 (cited as the Netherlands Draft). The Governors Draft was not published but was quoted and distributed widely; the Netherlands Draft of October 28 was published. (Another Netherlands Draft was issued on the eve of the Maastricht Summit but is not cited here. There were many other drafts of these documents, including one prepared in June 1991 by the Luxembourg Presidency, and some were quoted in the press, but they were not published and are not cited here.)

ahead to the conduct of monetary policy by the ECB and some of the problems it will face. The fourth chapter examines the role of fiscal policy in a monetary union and the corresponding provisions of the Treaty. The fifth chapter looks at the transitional arrangements, including the convergence criteria, the role of the European Monetary Institute (EMI), and the conduct of monetary and exchange-rate policies during the transition. The final chapter looks at EMU from outside—from the standpoint of the EC countries that will not enter right away, of other European countries, and of other major players in the international monetary system.[2] (Figure 1 describes the EC institutions involved in the development and management of EMU.)

Figure 1
EMU and the Institutions of the Community

Members of the *Commission* are appointed by their national governments but do not represent them; they serve as individuals. The Commission is the executive body of the EC but also initiates legislation by making proposals or recommendations to the *Council of Ministers,* which represents the member states. The Council must act unanimously on some matters (including decisions to amend proposals made by the Commission) but can act on other matters by qualified (weighted) majority voting. Certain decisions pertaining to EMU will require unanimity, and some of those are mentioned below. When Council meetings are attended by ministers of economics or finance, the Council is known as Ecofin. The Council of Ministers is different from the *European Council,* which is the formal name for the EC Summit. The European Council is attended by the heads of state or government and by the president of the Commission. It acts by "common accord" instead of formal voting. The ECB will have two councils of its own, a General Council and a Governing Council, and they will be cited by their full names here to minimize confusion; hence, references to the Council, without qualifying adjectives, pertain to the Council of Ministers.

The Maastricht Agreement increased the powers of the *European Parliament,* whose members are elected directly in each member country, but its role in EMU will be rather limited. The Council will have to "consult" the Parliament on many matters, and it will have to act in "cooperation" with the Parliament on some other matters. (Where "cooperation" is required, the Parliament can reject or amend a decision by the Council, but a unanimous vote of the Council can override an objection or amendment by the Parliament.) The main change in the powers of the Parliament made by the Maastricht Agreement—the requirement that the Parliament "assent" to certain decisions—crops up only rarely in those parts of the Treaty which deal with EMU. Certain parts of the ESCB Statute, for example, can be amended by the Council only after receiving the assent of the Parliament.

---

[2] The possibility of nonparticipation in the final stage of EMU has three roots: some countries may not be able to participate because they have not met the convergence criteria; new members of the EC may be subject to transitional arrangements; and the United Kingdom and Denmark may invoke the protocols that let them "opt out" of the final stage. The problems posed by nonparticipation will crop up at several points in this monograph.

Origins of EMU

The monetary history of the EC has two dimensions. Monetary cooperation began in the years right after the Second World War and intensified steadily thereafter. From time to time, however, efforts were made to accelerate the process—some by official bodies and some by academics.[3]

Monetary cooperation in Western Europe began long before the creation of the EC, with the establishment of the European Payments Union (EPU) in 1950, to multilateralize European trade and payments and provide a framework for moving to convertibility—a step taken at the end of 1958. Earlier in 1958, moreover, the EC had established a Monetary Committee to review economic and financial conditions, and it set up a Committee of Central Bank Governors in 1964, the only operational effect of a more ambitious plan drafted by the EC Commission in 1962, which looked to full-fledged monetary union by 1971.

The Werner Report

At the Hague Summit in 1969, however, the EC governments agreed to the gradual achievement of economic and monetary union, and they appointed Pierre Werner, Prime Minister and Finance Minister of Luxembourg, to chair a group of experts to draw up a detailed plan.

The Werner Report was completed in 1970 and called for the establishment of monetary union by 1980 (Figure 2). It made detailed recommendations for the first two stages of the process and described in more general terms the far-reaching reforms that would follow in the third stage. The first stage would take about three years and would focus on the coordination and convergence of monetary and fiscal policies; governments would formulate their national policies in the light of Community guidelines, and policy convergence would take place rapidly enough to obviate the need for exchange-rate changes in the second stage. Furthermore, exchange-rate fluctuations would be narrowed, and a fund for monetary cooperation would be established to provide short-term balance-of-payments credit to individual EC countries. Eventually, exchange rates would be fixed irreversibly, capital controls would be abolished, and an EC system of central banks, modeled on the US Federal Reserve System, would take over the conduct of monetary policy and of intervention on the foreign-exchange market. By that time, moreover, the size and financing of national budgets would be decided at the Community level by a body responsible to the European Parliament.[4]

---

[3] Ungerer et al. (1990) provide a detailed chronology, which I use heavily here. Note that I will not distinguish between the European Economic Community (EEC), established by the Treaty of Rome, and the whole group of Communities that now function together as the European Community (EC), with one Commission and one Council of Ministers.

[4] Baer and Padoa-Schioppa (1989) provide a critique of the Werner Report; see also Giovannini (1990).

In March 1971, the Council endorsed the strategy proposed by the Werner Report and took steps to implement some of its recommendations. In March 1972, exchange-rate fluctuations were reduced by limiting the swings in bilateral exchange rates to a $2\frac{1}{4}$ percent band; the arrangement was known as the "snake in the tunnel" because it made the participating currencies move up and down together within the wider $4\frac{1}{2}$ percent band established for the dollar by the Smithsonian Agreement of 1971. But the worldwide shift to floating exchange rates in March 1973 abolished the tunnel, allowing the snake to undulate freely, and this made it more costly for some countries to participate. They began to drop away, letting their currencies float independently.

Figure 2.
The Chronology of European Monetary Union

October 1970	Final report by Werner Committee
March 1971	Council endorses achievement by 1980 of economic and monetary union
March 1972	European "snake" established, surrounding EC exchange rates by narrow band
April 1973	European Monetary Cooperation Fund established
July 1978	Bremen meeting of European Council endorses plan for European Monetary System
March 1979	European Monetary System begins to operate
February 1986	Signing of Single European Act aimed at completing internal market by 1992
June 1988	Hanover meeting of European Council establishes Delors Committee
April 1989	Delors Committee publishes report
June 1989	Madrid meeting of European Council agrees that Stage One of EMU will start on July 1, 1990 and calls for IGC to work on subsequent stages
October 1990	Rome meeting of European Council, with UK dissenting, agrees that Stage Two of EMU should start on January 1 1994
December 1990	Beginning of intergovernmental conferences on EMU and political union
December 1990	Maastricht meeting of European Council adopts amendments to Treaty of Rome on EMU and political union, including procedures and framework for establishing ESCB and ECB

In April 1973, the Council established the European Monetary Cooperation Fund (EMCF), adopting another recommendation made by the Werner Report. And in February 1974, the Council agreed to draft annual policy guidelines of the sort recommended by the Werner Report for policy coordination and convergence.

But divergence, not convergence, was happening everywhere, because of the ways in which economies and governments were adapting to the oil shock of 1973-74. Inflation rates were rising, but at different speeds, and so were unemployment rates. For the next few years, indeed, the concerns and energies of European governments focused on immediate economic problems rather than the long-term future. And when they resumed work on European monetary integration, they abandoned the agenda of the Werner Report, to respond to the call by Helmut Schmidt of Germany and Valery Giscard D'Estaing of France to create a "zone of monetary stability in Europe" by establishing a European Monetary System (EMS).

The European Monetary System

The Schmidt-Giscard proposal was endorsed by the Bremen Summit in July 1978, the main features of the EMS were defined by the Council in December, and an agreement among the EC central banks brought the system into being in March 1979.

The EMS was meant to be a more flexible, symmetrical version of the Bretton Woods System, which had governed global exchange-rate arrangements from the end of the Second World War until the move to floating exchange rates in 1973. Each country participating in the Exchange Rate Mechanism (ERM) of the EMS must keep the exchange rate for its currency within a band defined by a grid of central rates for the various pairs of currencies. When an exchange rate reaches the edge of its band, both countries concerned are obliged to intervene on the foreign-exchange market to prevent the rate from going further. But they have unlimited access to the short-term credit facilities of the EMCF whenever they require a partner country's currency for this sort of intervention.[5] The central rates can be revised with the consent of all concerned, and there have been twelve realignments, some of them involving several currencies at once.

Eight EC countries joined the ERM initially, but one of them, Italy, was allowed to adopt a wide 6 percent band for its currency instead of the narrow $2\frac{1}{4}$ percent band carried over from the snake. Spain joined the ERM in June 1989, and the United Kingdom followed in October 1990, both of them with wide bands. But Italy moved to the narrow band in

---

5 In practice, EC central banks have intervened more frequently *within* the bands than at the limits, and they cannot count on automatic access to EMCF credit lines for financing intramarginal intervention. On the practices and evolution of the EMS, see Gros and Thygesen (1988), Giavazzi and Giovannini (1989), and Ungerer et al. (1990).

January 1990. The two other EC countries, Greece and Portugal, have not yet joined the ERM.

The European Currency Unit (ECU) was meant to play a major role in the EMS. It is defined as a basket of EC currencies and is the accounting unit of the EMS.[6] But the ECU has played a larger role in international financial markets than in the EMS itself. EC institutions, national governments, and corporations borrow in ECU; banks accept ECU deposits; and a transnational clearing system has been developed to settle ECU-denominated claims. Under the new Treaty, moreover, the ECU will become a currency in its own right—the single currency of the monetary union.

There were several realignments in the early years of the EMS, as the member countries sought by trial and error to offset inherited cost and price disparities, as well as the additional cost and price disparities produced by differences between the members' policies—including their responses to the second oil shock. The early realignments, moreover, "were generally agreed without much critical introspection and were not accompanied by comprehensive domestic stabilization measures" (Ungerer et al., 1990, p. 2).

This early phase was ended dramatically, however, in March 1983, when the Mitterrand government in France abandoned domestic expansion in favor of rigorous stabilization. There was a comprehensive realignment at that point, and there have been far fewer realignments since. In fact, the ERM has been transformed into a virtual deutsche mark zone, as France, Italy, and other member countries have "borrowed credibility" from the Bundesbank by committing themselves firmly to exchange-rate stability and using that commitment as the rationale for following domestic monetary policies aimed at price stability.[7] This change in the nature of the EMS was ratified tacitly by the Basle-Nyborg Agreement of September 1987, in which the central banks of the ERM countries agreed "to the use of interest-rate differentials to defend the stability of the EMS parity grid" and thus to tie their own interest-rate policies to those of the Bundesbank.[8]

---

[6] An ECU consists of 0.624 deutsche marks, 1.33 French francs, 152 lira, 0.0878 pounds, and so on, and Article 109g of the Treaty will fix its currency composition until the final stage of EMU, when the ECU as basket will give way to the ECU as currency. Under the 1978 Council resolution on the establishment of the EMS, the ECU was to be the reserve asset of the European Monetary Fund (EMF), which would replace the EMCF and serve as the institutional home of the EMS. But that plan died quietly.

[7] See Giavazzi and Pagano (1988). Although there is widespread agreement with this characterization of the transformation in the EMS, the econometric evidence is mixed; see, e.g., Weber (1991). Furthermore, there is disagreement on the extent to which participation in the ERM has contributed to the pursuit of price stability. Collins (1988) and De Grauwe (1989a, 1989b) find little evidence to this effect, but Ungerer et al. (1986), Giavazzi and Giovannini (1988, 1989), and Artis and Nachane (1989) find some EMS effects. For more on these matters, see the survey by Haldane (1991).

[8] For its part, the Bundesbank agreed to the more liberal use of EMCF credit lines for intramarginal intervention, in exchange for a commitment by the other central banks to make fuller use of the

As governments and others began to view the EMS as a fixed-rate regime, or very nearly so, the case for going further—all the way to EMU—became more appealing, and it was supported by two considerations. Both were linked to the signing of the Single European Act in 1986 and the decision to complete the internal market by the end of 1992.

- The decision to complete the internal market lent new force to the belief long held by many Europeans that closely integrated national economies like those of the EC have more to gain from exchange-rate stability than from occasional exchange-rate realignments. It was argued, indeed, that the EC countries could not capture the full gains from the internal market unless they went on to eliminate the exchange-rate uncertainties and conversion costs produced by using separate national currencies. The strongest statement of this view was made later on, in the Commission's brief for EMU, aptly titled "One Market, One Money" (Commission, 1990).

- Among the first steps taken to complete the single market was the decision in June 1988 to require the lifting of all capital controls by July 1990. Once those controls were gone, however, doubts about the fixity of ERM exchange rates might generate speculative capital movements large enough to force exchange-rate realignments or, at least, to interfere with the normal course of monetary policy. This concern was put most vividly by Padoa-Schioppa, who warned against trying to reconcile an "inconsistent quartet" of policy objectives: free trade, full capital mobility, fixed exchange rates, and independent national monetary policies. "In the long run," he said, "the only solution to the inconsistency is to complement the internal market with a monetary union" (Padoa-Schioppa, 1988, p. 376).[9]

These two arguments were frequently combined in a less sophisticated but more pointed way. It is fine for us to follow the Bundesbank when fighting inflation is our paramount concern, but can we afford to follow it over the longer run, when seeking to create jobs for a growing labor force? If Europe is to have a common monetary policy, by choice or necessity, shouldn't it be provided by a European institution responsive to the needs of Europe as a whole? Ironically, the process started by the asking of this

---

exchange-rate bands and thus avoid "prolonged bouts" of intramarginal intervention. The phrases quoted here and in the text come from the Council's communiqué of September 12, 1987.

[9] This argument, though popular and quite persuasive, was perhaps put too strongly. Capital controls did not prevent speculative crises in the early 1980s, and the dismantling of controls, which began before the 1990 deadline, did not produce speculative crises. Furthermore, the open-ended credit facilities of the EMCF may have been far more important than capital controls in curbing speculative pressures; see Kenen (1988). Finally, there were other ways to resolve the dilemma posed by Padoa-Schioppa; see Driffill (1988), Gros and Thygesen (1988), Kenen (1988), and Russo and Tullio (1988), who proposed ways to make small exchange-rate changes that would not induce massive capital movements and threaten the stability of the EMS.

question—the process that led to the Maastricht Agreement—will produce an institution that may not be very responsive to the needs and aspirations of those who posed the question. But that is to get far ahead of our story.

The Delors Report

The first official response to the revival of interest in EMU was taken by the Hanover Summit in June 1988. Reaffirming the Community's commitment to the "progressive realization of economic and monetary union," it appointed a committee, chaired by Jacques Delors, President of the Commission, to propose "concrete stages" that would lead toward EMU.[10] The Delors Committee was asked to report to the Madrid Summit in June 1989.

The Worlds of the Werner and Delors Reports

Before reviewing the recommendations of the Delors Report, it is perhaps worth mentioning four major differences between the world of 1969-70, in which the Werner Committee worked, and the world of 1988-89, in which the Delors Committee worked. These help to explain the differences between their reports and, perhaps, the difference in their ultimate impact.[11]

In 1969-70, the world was losing faith in fixed exchange rates, and the collapse of the Bretton Woods System was not far away. Although the Werner Report had recommended a narrowing of exchange-rate fluctuations, governments were starting to question their ability to keep exchange rates fixed over any long period of time.[12] In 1988-89, by contrast, Europe was completing a decade of experience with the EMS, which was looking more and more like a fixed-rate system. Furthermore, many Europeans were coming to believe that exchange-rate changes within Europe were no longer necessary or desirable.

In 1969-70, most EC countries were still using capital controls and were far from ready to abandon them. The United Kingdom was among the first to end them but did not do so until 1979. Hence, the Werner Report did not insist on eliminating capital controls and integrating European capital markets early in the process leading to EMU. By 1988-89, by contrast, most of the controls were gone, and there was a deadline for

---

[10] The Committee consisted of the twelve central bank governors and five other experts. All of them acted as individuals and all of them signed the Committee's report. The Committee has been accused of focusing too narrowly on the methods for achieving EMU, without making an adequate case for EMU. The Committee is careful to point out, however, that this was its mandate.

[11] Giovannini (1990) makes some of these same points.

[12] Although the world was much further from full capital mobility in 1969-70, there was enough to generate large speculative flows, and Padoa-Schioppa's warning about the "inconsistent quartet" could have been uttered even then. Cooper (1968) said much the same thing.

removing the rest. Furthermore, the Commission was already working on legislation, including the Second Banking Directive, to unify European capital markets. Thus, much of the work needed for economic union was already under way, not part of the long-term agenda, and the Delors Committee could concentrate more narrowly on the mandate and design of a monetary union. Equally important, the Delors Committee could argue with some confidence that capital movements—and even labor movements—would contribute to balance-of-payments adjustment among the EC countries and thus compensate them partially for giving up control over their own interest rates and exchange rates. The Werner Report could promise that factor mobility would contribute to adjustment in the distant future but not early on in EMU.

In 1969-70, Europe had less settled views about the appropriate division of powers between the Community and its members. France, for example, still strongly opposed any transfer of sovereignty to EC institutions. Hence, the Werner Report stirred up strong opposition when it called for early limits on national autonomy in monetary and fiscal matters. There is still disagreement, of course, about the appropriate division of responsibilities, and it arose at Maastricht. But much of the debate today relates to the new areas—foreign, defense, and social policies—not to the old area of economic policy. The principle of *subsidiarity* has been well defined and broadly accepted; the Community should not take on tasks which national or local governments can perform with greater or equal effectiveness. The principle may have kept the Delors Committee from proposing more effective fiscal-policy arrangements, an issue discussed in Chapter IV below, but likewise protected it from being too ambitious.

Finally, the Phillips Curve was still alive and well in 1969-70, and "fine tuning" was a goal, not a term of ridicule. It was possible, we thought, to choose between unemployment and inflation and to make the choice effective by adjusting monetary and fiscal policies.[13] And these views were reflected in the Werner Report:

> The procedures for policy coordination detailed in the Report implies a very high degree of confidence in the ability of policy instruments to affect policy goals in a known and predictable way. This over-optimistic view of the efficacy of economic management gave rise to a rather mechanistic and relatively rigid approach to policy coordination (Baer and Padoa-Schioppa, 1989, p. 57).

While many economists continue to believe that monetary and fiscal policies have important roles to play in improving economic performance and stability, few would be prepared to predict precisely the size and speed of the response to any change in policy. There is broad agreement

---

[13] See Corden (1972), whose critique of the case for European monetary union was based in part on the belief that countries have different Phillips Curves and different policy preferences. Such differences, he argued, would raise the costs of sacrificing monetary independence.

in Europe, moreover, on the importance of price stability, on the need to dedicate monetary policy to that basic aim, and on the need to insulate central banks from any interference with the pursuit of price stability. It was thus fairly easy for the Delors Committee to define the mandate and draft the constitution of the central-banking system for the final stage of EMU.

What EMU Would Mean

The Delors Report began by setting out the basic requirements of EMU. Citing the Werner Report, it listed three necessary conditions for a monetary union: the total convertibility of currencies, the complete liberalization of capital flows and full integration of financial markets, and the irrevocable locking of exchange rates. The first and second requirements, it noted, are already met in Europe. By meeting the third, the EC would become a single currency area, but it should probably go further:[14]

> The adoption of a *single currency*, while not strictly necessary for the creation of a monetary union, might be seen—for economic as well as psychological and political reasons—as a natural and desirable further development of the monetary union. A single currency would clearly demonstrate the irreversibility of the...monetary union, considerably facilitate the monetary management of the Community and avoid the transactions costs of converting currencies.... The replacement of national currencies by a single currency should therefore take place as soon as possible after the locking of parities [23].

The establishment of a monetary union, however, would have far-reaching implications for monetary policy:

> Once permanently fixed exchange rates had been adopted, there would be a *need for a common monetary policy*, which would be carried out through new operating procedures. The coordination of...national monetary policies...would not be sufficient. The responsibility for the single monetary policy would have to be vested in a new institution, in which centralized and collective decisions would be taken on the supply of money and credit as well as on other instruments of monetary policy, including interest rates. This shift from national monetary policies to a single monetary policy is an inescapable consequence of monetary union and constitutes one of the principal institutional changes [24].

But steps are needed in three domains to avoid or correct economic imbalances: competition policy and other measures to strengthen market mechanisms; common policies to enhance the process of resource allocation where market forces are not adequate; and macroeconomic coordination, including binding rules in the budgetary field.

---

[14] All of the quotations in this and the next sub-section come from the Delors Report (1989), and the numbers in brackets refer to the paragraphs of the report. All italics appear in the original.

The Committee's recommendations concerning competition and resource allocation lie beyond the scope of this monograph, but its comments on fiscal policies deserve close attention. The Committee began by stressing the need for mutually consistent and sound behavior:

> In particular, uncoordinated and divergent national budgetary policies would undermine monetary stability and generate imbalances in the real and financial sectors of the Community. Moreover, the fact that the centrally managed Community budget is likely to remain a very small part of total public-sector spending and that much of this budget will not be available for cyclical adjustments will mean that the task of setting a Community-wide fiscal policy stance will have to be performed through the coordination of national budgetary policies. Without such coordination it would be impossible for the Community as a whole to establish a fiscal/monetary policy mix appropriate for the preservation of internal balance, or for the Community to play its part in the international adjustment process [30].

It went on to argue that markets can discipline governments to some extent but tend to operate erratically; they lend too freely, then shut down abruptly. Accordingly, it made two sets of recommendations:

> In the general macroeconomic field, a common overall assessment of ... economic developments in the Community would need to be agreed periodically and would constitute the framework for a better coordination of national economic policies. The Community would need to monitor its overall economic situati]n, to assess the consistency of developments in individual countries with regard to common objectives and formulate guidelines for policy [30].

And then these stronger recommendations:

> In the budgetary field, binding rules are required that would: firstly, impose effective upper limits on budget deficits of individual member countries of the Community, although ... the situation of each member country might have to be taken into consideration; secondly, exclude access to direct central bank credit and other forms of monetary financing while, however, permitting open market operations in government securities; thirdly, limit recourse to external borrowing in non-Community currencies [30].

Most of these recommendations found their way to Maastricht, apart from the one about external borrowing, which got lost along the way. But the weak ones got weaker and the strong ones stronger.

Returning to the need for a single monetary policy, the Delors Report made its most important recommendation:

> A new monetary institution would be needed because a single monetary policy cannot result from independent decisions and actions by different central banks. Moreover, day-to-day monetary policy operations cannot respond quickly to changing market conditions unless they are decided

centrally. Considering the political structure of the Community and the advantages of making existing central banks part of a new system, the domestic and international monetary policy-making of the Community should be organized in a federal form, in what might be called a *European System of Central Banks* (ESCB). ... [It] could consist of a central institution (with its own balance sheet) and the national central banks. At the final stage the ESCB—acting through its Council—would be responsible for formulating and implementing monetary policy as well as managing the Community's exchange rate policy vis-à-vis third currencies. The national central banks would be entrusted with the implementation of policies in conformity with guidelines established by the Council of the ESCB and in accordance with instructions from the central institution [32].

The European System of Central Banks would have a four-fold mandate:

- The System would be committed to the objective of price stability;

- Subject to the foregoing, the System should support the general economic policy set at the Community level by the competent bodies;

- The System would be responsible for the formulation and implementation of monetary policy, exchange rate and reserve management, and the maintenance of a properly functioning payment system;

- The System would participate in the coordination of banking supervision policies of the supervisory authorities [32].

Most of these recommendations also found their way to Maastricht, along with the Committee's recommendations concerning the organization, powers, and independence of the ESCB (and there is no reason to recite them here, because we will examine them in their final form).

How to Get to EMU

Like the Werner Committee before it, the Delors Committee outlined a three-stage process for reaching EMU but was more specific about each stage and the links between them. After some general observations and a few rather tentative comments about the role of the ECU, it set out its timetable.

Stage One of EMU would initiate the process. In the economic field, it would see the completion of the internal market, the reform and enlargement of the Community's structural funds in order to reduce regional disparities within the EC, and the introduction of a comprehensive framework for policy surveillance and coordination using agreed indicators. For fiscal policies, in particular, coordination would employ "precise quantitative guidelines" and "provide for concerted budgetary action by the member countries" [51]. In the monetary field, Stage One would see the removal of all obstacles to financial integration and an intensification of monetary coordination.[15] All of the EC currencies would enter the exchange-rate mechanism of the EMS, and EC governments would remove any remaining impediments to private use of the ECU. "Realignments of exchange rates would still be possible, but an effort would be made by every country to make the functioning of other adjustment mechanisms more effective" [52].[16]

Stage Two of EMU would involve important innovations. In the economic field, policy surveillance would be strengthened, and precise rules would be set to limit national budget deficits. (The Commission would bring to the attention of the Council instances of noncompliance and would propose remedial action when necessary, but the rules would not be binding until Stage Three.) Furthermore, the Community as a single entity would take an active role in international discussions on exchange-rate matters and policy coordination. But the largest innovations would occur in the monetary field. The ESCB would be established, take over the tasks of the EMCF and the Committee of Central Bank Governors, and begin the move from the coordination of national monetary policies to the design and implementation of a common monetary policy. The Delors Committee recognized frankly the problems involved in this sort of transition but was not prepared to propose a detailed blueprint. Nevertheless, it tried to identify some steps that might be taken. For example,

> ...general monetary orientations would be set for the Community as a whole, with an understanding that national monetary policy would be executed in accordance with these global guidelines. Moreover, while the ultimate responsibility for monetary policy decisions would remain with national authorities, the operational framework necessary for deciding and implementing a common monetary policy would be created and experimented with. Also, a certain amount of exchange reserves would be pooled and would be used to conduct exchange market interventions in accordance with guidelines established by the ESCB Council. Finally, regulatory functions would be exercised by the ESCB in the monetary and banking field in order to achieve a minimum harmonization of provisions (such as reserve requirements or payment

---

15 The Committee went on to recommend specific changes in the mandate of the Committee of Central Bank Governors. It would be consulted in advance on national decisions about monetary policies, such as the setting of monetary targets; it could express opinions to individual governments on matters of Community-wide concern; and its chairman could decide to make its opinions public. The Delors Committee also suggested "extending the scope of central banks' autonomy" [52]. It was agreed at Maastricht, however, that no action on this matter would have to be taken before Stage Three. The reason will become apparent in Chapter V, which will compare the timetable in the Delors Report with the one in the new Treaty.

16 Several members of the Delors Committee wanted to create a European Reserve Fund, which would foreshadow the future ESCB by managing some of the reserves of the EC countries and, possibly, intervening on foreign-exchange markets; other members objected, however, that an institution of this sort, focused mainly on foreign-exchange operations, would not really foreshadow the ESCB. (What was really foreshadowed at this point was the debate in the weeks before Maastricht on the functions and powers of the EMI.)

arrangements) necessary for the future conduct of a common monetary policy [57].

The ERM exchange-rate band might be narrowed in Stage Two, and realignments would be made only in exceptional circumstances.

Stage Three of EMU would begin with the irrevocable locking of exchange rates, and the ESCB would assume full control over the conduct of monetary policy. Eventually, a single currency would be issued to replace the members' national currencies. Official reserves would be transferred to the ESCB, which would be responsible for intervention vis-à-vis third currencies "in accordance with Community exchange rate policy" [60]. Finally, the fiscal rules would take full effect and would be enforced by the Council, in cooperation with the European Parliament [59].

The Road to Maastricht

In June 1989, the Madrid Summit received the Delors Report and decided that Stage One of EMU should begin in July 1990. In December 1989, the Strasbourg Summit decided to convene an Intergovernmental Conference (IGC) in December 1990 to work on the subsequent stages. In June 1990, moreover, the Dublin Summit decided to convene *two* such conferences—one on EMU and one on political union—and asked them to finish their work in time for ratification of amendments to the Treaty by the end of 1992, the deadline for completing the internal market. The Committee of Central Bank Governors was asked to draft a statute for the ESCB in preparation for the IGC on EMU.

These decisions appear to reflect widespread acceptance of the Delors Report, but basic disagreements developed right away. Some governments wanted to complete EMU quickly; they believed that rapid institutional change would induce the necessary adaptations in economic policies and performance. Other governments wanted economic convergence to take place before creation of the ECB; they believed that this would protect the ECB against political pressures from countries that had failed to reduce their inflation rates and might want the ECB to pursue a monetary policy less stringent than required to maintain price stability.[17] The first view, held by France and Italy, endorsed the recommendation made in the Delors Report that the ECB should be created in Stage Two because it would maintain political momentum. The second view, held by Germany and the Netherlands, questioned that recommendation, because it might allow institutional change to get ahead of economic convergence.

---

[17] The two views are set forth succinctly by Gros and Thygesen and by Vaubel in Greenaway, ed. (1990). The same debate took place at the time of the Werner Report; see Giovannini (1990).

Those who held this second view, moreover, opposed any gradual transfer of responsibility for monetary policy during Stage Two. The Delors Report, they said, had been inconsistent; while arguing at times for the gradual transfer of operational authority, it had also acknowledged the indivisibility of operational responsibility.[18]

The United Kingdom raised fundamental questions about the ultimate aims of EMU. It strongly supported the completion of the internal market and the integration of financial markets but not the creation of an ECB at some fixed date in the future or the introduction of a single currency. Therefore, it agreed to the beginning of Stage One but favored an "evolutionary approach" thereafter (H.M. Treasury, 1989). It also opposed binding rules on national budget deficits. Later on, it introduced a proposal of its own, involving the creation of a European Monetary Fund to issue a "hard ECU" in exchange for national currencies. The hard ECU could never be devalued against the other EC currencies, and it would compete for favor in the private sector. If successful in this competition, it would gradually become the common currency of the EC and might even become the single currency in the longer run.[19]

These issues were debated at the Rome Summit in October 1990, where eleven of the twelve EC governments agreed to start Stage Two in January 1994 and went on to list the steps that would be taken in Stage Three. Exchange rates would be irrevocably locked, there would be a single currency, and "a new monetary institution" would exercise full responsibility for the conduct of monetary policy, with price stability as its aim. It would be independent but would report to "institutions that are politically responsible." But the governments pointedly refrained from endorsing any transfer of responsibility during Stage Two; the new institution, they said, would coordinate national monetary policies, develop the instruments needed in Stage Three to conduct a single monetary policy, and oversee the development of the ECU. Furthermore, they declined to say anything about the role of the new institution in bank supervision. Finally, they agreed that the starting date for Stage Three would depend on the degree of convergence achieved in the previous stages. In short, more points for Dutch and German views than for French and Italian views.

And fewer points for the United Kingdom, whose dissenting views were set out separately at the end of the communiqué. While endorsing many of the basic objectives set forth in the communiqué, the United Kingdom was unable to accept the other governments' approach to EMU.

---

[18] See Crockett (1991a) for an excellent discussion of this issue.

[19] See H.M. Treasury (1991) and Crockett (1991b). This was not the first plan to use a "parallel currency" as a device for moving gradually to ECU. Several economists made a similar proposal, less fully articulated, in the "All Saints' Day Manifesto for European Monetary Union" published in *The Economist* on November 1, 1975.

15

It was ready to move beyond Stage One by creating a new monetary institution and a common currency, but the use of the word "common" rather than "single" was meant to differentiate its plan for a hard ECU from the recommendations of the Delors Report.

When the IGC convened a few weeks later, many questions had still to be settled. Four of them pertained to Stage Three: (1) Should excessive budget deficits be prohibited and, if so, what sorts of sanctions would most effective? (2) How should the Community make exchange-rate policy, and how much autonomy should the ECB enjoy in the execution of that policy? (3) To what extent should the ECB be involved in prudential supervision? (4) How should the independence of the ECB be protected and how should its accountability be defined?

All of these questions were answered by the IGC before it reported to the Maastricht Summit. But equally difficult questions had to be decided about Stage Two and the transition to Stage Three: Should the ECB be created at the start of Stage Two to plan and manage the transition to monetary union, or should those tasks be given to another institution? How and when should the EC decide to start Stage Three and what should that decision mean for individual countries? Should a country be excluded from the ECB for failing to achieve enough convergence, or should convergence be employed as a general criterion for deciding when Stage Three should start? Should all eligible countries have to join the ECB, or should a country be permitted to "opt out" of the monetary union? Where should the ECB have its home?

Some of these questions were also answered by the ICG, but two of them had to be answered at Maastricht—the rules for deciding to start Stage Three and whether individual countries could opt out. And the home of the ECB has not yet been chosen. In early drafts of the ESCB Statute, Article 37 read in full: "The seat of the ECB shall be established at (..)." But the Netherlands Draft of October 28 made a small change: "The seat of the ECB shall be established at (.........)," which led to much counting of letters on fingers: Amsterdam or Frankfurt? Edinburgh perhaps? Or maybe Barcelona? The Maastricht Summit decided that the seats of the EMI and ECB should be chosen before the end of 1992.

The outcome at Maastricht remained in doubt, however, because of issues coming from the other IGC. Germany would not agree to EMU without obtaining the closer political union to which it was committed. The United Kingdom would not accept an EC social policy. But agreement was reached in the final moments of the Maastricht Summit, thanks to the remarkable political momentum acquired by a process that had started rather modestly in 1988, when the Hanover Summit created the Delors Committee.

II. The ESCB and ECB

What will happen in Stage Three, when the ECB acquires responsibility for making monetary policy? What will be its mandate? How will it formulate and implement policy? How independent will it be?

These questions are examined in this and the next chapter. This chapter looks at the constitution of the ECB; the next chapter looks at operational problems. Before turning to these matters, however, consider the decisions taken by the Intergovernmental Conference (IGC) and the Maastricht Summit concerning the procedure for moving to Stage Three.

When Stage Three Will Start

Early in its work, the IGC decided to create *two* new institutions. One will be established at the start of Stage Two, in January 1994, to coordinate national monetary policies and manage the transition to monetary union. It will be known as the European Monetary Institute (EMI), and its tasks are examined in Chapter V. The other institution is the ECB, which will be established just before Stage Three begins. Furthermore, the IGC adopted strict convergence criteria, not merely to decide if and when Stage Three should start, but also to decide which countries can participate.

These decisions were embodied in a draft of the Treaty prepared by the Netherlands Presidency of the IGC, which also included an opt-out clause of the sort proposed by the United Kingdom. Although it was not fully acceptable to any EC government, it described the direction in which the IGC appeared to be heading six weeks before the Maastricht Summit.

The Netherlands Draft

The transitional provisions of the Netherlands Draft instructed the Commission and EMI to report to the Council by the end of 1996 on the progress made by member states in meeting their obligations with regard to EMU and on "the achievement of a high degree of sustainable convergence" as measured by specific quantitative criteria.[1] The Commission and EMI were also told to report on the development of the ECU, the integration of markets, the state of current-account balances, and the evolution of unit labor costs and other price indexes.[2] The Council would then decide which member states "fulfil the necessary conditions for the adoption of a single currency" and recommend its findings to the European Council. Taking account of these findings and the opinion of the European Parliament, the European Council would then assess whether it was appropriate to begin Stage Three and, if so, on what date. If it could not agree on a date, the whole process would be repeated periodically thereafter.

An affirmative finding by the European Council would trigger formal action by the Council of Ministers to fix the date for starting Stage Three and decide which countries were ready to participate. Those that were not, because they had failed to meet the convergence criteria, would be granted "derogations" from their obligations under various provisions of the Treaty. But the Council could not force any country to participate in Stage Three if that country's parliament did not "feel free to approve of the irrevocable fixing of its currency" at the beginning of Stage Three. Such a country would be granted an "exemption" with effects similar to a derogation.[3] If the number of countries without derogations or exemptions was sufficiently large, the Council would confirm the starting date for Stage Three.

These elaborate procedures were endorsed initially by Germany and other countries wanting to make sure that Stage Three would not start unless there was convergence, and they were likewise acceptable to the United Kingdom—the country most likely to seek an exemption. But France and Italy were not happy with them.[4] A French friend put their view this way:

---

1 The criteria themselves are discussed in Chapter V.

2 The same list appears in Article 109j of the text adopted at Maastricht.

3 Countries with a derogation or exemption would not be able to vote in the Council of Ministers or in the Governing Council of the ECB on matters pertaining to monetary policy or to the Community's exchange-rate policy for the single currency. Biennially, if not more often, the Council would decide whether countries with derogations were ready to participate, and a country with an exemption could ask at any time for its exemption to be terminated.

4 So were the other countries of the Southern Tier—Spain, Portugal, and Greece—which did not want to be excluded from Stage Three for failing to meet the convergence criteria, and their concerns were not allayed by the procedure adopted at Maastricht. But Spain succeeded in obtaining an agreement to reform the EC budget, provide more regional assistance, and set up a "cohesion fund" to finance environmental projects and trans-European transport networks.

We began with a plan for monetary union—the Delors Report. We wound up with a set of rules for deciding in the future whether to establish a monetary union. Instead of charting a pathway to EMU, the IGC has laid out an obstacle course. Worse yet, the finish line may not stand still. It can drift indefinitely into the next century.

Pessimists warned, moreover, that Britain might not the only country to seek an exemption. Germany might want one too, and EMU without Germany would not be viable.[5]

The French Proposal
In an effort to make sure that Stage Three would start before the end of the Twentieth Century and not be postponed indefinitely, France made a new proposal in the final hours of the IGC, and it was accepted at Maastricht. Stage Three will begin automatically in January 1999 if there is no agreement to start it earlier, and Germany will not be able to opt out.

Under the transitional provisions adopted at Maastricht and summarized in Figure 3, the process will start as before. The Commission and the EMI will report to the Council on the state of readiness for Stage Three. The Council, acting by a qualified majority, will assess whether each EC country meets the conditions necessary for adopting a single currency and whether a majority does so. It will then recommend its findings to an unusual meeting of the Council attended by heads of state or government. Taking account of the reports by the Commission and the EMI, the assessment by the Council, and the opinion of the Parliament, that meeting will decide whether a majority of EC countries is ready to adopt a single currency and whether it is appropriate to start Stage Three. If so, it will set the date.

This process must be completed by the end of 1996 and resembles the one proposed in the Netherlands Draft. But now the crucial innovation:

> If by the end of 1997 the date for the beginning of the third stage has not been set, the third stage shall start on 1 January 1999.

No ifs, buts, or maybes. There will be more reports and recommendations, and another special meeting of the Council. But that meeting will have merely to decide which countries meet the necessary conditions, so that the others can be granted derogations under Article 109k. That article resembles the one in the Netherlands Draft, but it has no opt-out clause. Instead, two protocols are attached to the Treaty, for Britain and Denmark, allowing them to opt out of Stage Three.[6]

---

5 This concern may explain why Germany itself backed away from the idea, even before the German press began to attack EMU. (Shortly before Maastricht, *Bild Zeitung* ran a banner headline, "The Mark To Be Abolished", and went on in this vein for several days, citing opinion polls lopsidedly opposed to EMU; *Financial Times*, December 6 and 12, 1991.)

6 The UK protocol recognizes that "the United Kingdom shall not be obliged or committed to move to the third stage of Economic and Monetary Union without a separate decision to do so by its government and Parliament." The Danish protocol notes that a referendum may be needed before Denmark can participate in Stage Three and grants Denmark an exemption if it cannot participate.

Thus, the French proposal adopted at Maastricht guarantees the advent of Stage Three by a method far more certain than the one in the Delors Report. Although the ECB will not be established at the beginning of Stage Two to work for the early arrival of Stage Three, there is no way to keep Stage Three from starting in 1999 unless the EC countries agree unanimously to amend the Treaty after having ratified it.[7]

Figure 3.
Schedule for Stages Two and Three

January 1, 1994	Stage Two starts
	EMI established
	Bans on monetary financing and bailouts take effect
	Ban on excessive deficits takes effect (but no sanctions until Stage Three)
December 31, 1996	EMI specifies framework for ESCB
	EC Council decides if majority of EC countries meets necessary conditions for adopting single currency and if it is appropriate to start Stage Three. If so, it sets a starting date for Stage Three. If not, Stage Three starts automatically on January 1, 1999
Before Stage Three starts	ECB Board chosen, ECB established, and EMI liquidated
	EC Council approves enabling legislation for ESCB
	Countries not ready for Stage Three granted derogations
When Stage Three starts	Exchange rates irrevocably locked
	ECB assumes responsibility for monetary policy

How Stage Three Will Start

As soon as the starting date for Stage Three has been set, and no later than July 1998, three steps will be taken:

- The Executive Board of the ECB will be appointed—the president, vice-president, and four other members. They will be chosen by "common accord" of the EC governments participating in Stage Three, on the recommendation of the Council and after consulting the European Parliament and the Governing Council of the ECB. Their terms will normally last 8 years and will not be renewable. On this

---

[7] There may be one other way to postpone Stage Three—by deciding before 1998 to start Stage Three on a date later than 1 January 1999. (It should be noted that Germany did not object to the French proposal, despite its previous insistence on convergence as a requirement for starting Stage Three. But Germany made many concessions at Maastricht.)

first round, however, the Vice-President will serve for 4 years and the four other members for 5 to 8 years, so that the membership of the Board will rotate gradually in the future.[8]

- The ECB will be established as soon as the Executive Board has been appointed and will exercise its powers from the first day of Stage Three.[9]

- The Council will adopt the legislation required by various articles of the ESCB Statute. These pertain, *inter alia*, to the terms on which the ECB may impose reserve requirements, its right to call up additional foreign-exchange reserves from the national central banks, the issuance of regulations by the ECB, and the scope of its advisory functions.[10]

On the first day of Stage Three, the Council, acting unanimously on a proposal from the Commission and after consulting the ECB, will adopt the conversion rates at which the participating countries' currencies will be irrevocably fixed and the rates at which the ECU will replace them, "and the ECU will become a currency in its own right." This decision, however, must not modify the external value of the ECU. The Council will also take the measures required to introduce the ECU as the single currency of the Community.[11]

It will take a long time to substitute the ECU for the participants' national currencies. Every coin-using machine must be modified, and all sorts of menus must be rewritten—from simple lists of retail prices to stock-exchange quotations. Thousands of computer programs must be amended.[12] Fewer changes are needed, however, at the "wholesale" level. The ECB could do all of its business in ECU from the first day of Stage

---

8 Articles 11 and 50 of the ESCB Statute. On this first occasion, the governments will consult the Council of the EMI, as the Governing Council of the ECB will not yet exist. Directors of the Bundesbank also serve for 8-year terms, but these are renewable, and actual terms of office have averaged from 10 to 12 years (Kennedy, 1991, p. 16). Governors of the Federal Reserve System have 14-year terms, but actual terms have been shorter because of resignations and because new governors are appointed to fill the unexpired terms of those who resign before their terms expire.

9 Article 109l of the Treaty. As the ECB will take over the functions of the EMI, the latter will be liquidated as soon as the ECB is established.

10 Articles 106 and 109l of the Treaty. The Council will act by qualified majority and consult the European Parliament, but may follow either one of two procedures; it may act on a proposal from the Commission and consult the ECB, or act on a recommendation from the ECB and consult the Commission. There is a small oddity here. Countries that do not participate in Stage Three may not vote in the Council on most matters involving the ECB, but they are not kept from voting on this legislation. (See Article 109k of the Treaty, which limits the voting rights of nonparticipants but does not mention Article 109l.)

11 Article 109l of the Treaty. I will argue in Chapter V that the language quoted in the text permits a final realignment of EMS exchange rates.

12 The introduction of the ECU will be made harder by the fact that no EC currency is equal in value to a convenient multiple or fraction of the ECU, and it is impossible to round up or down without realigning exchange rates significantly. Giovannini (1991) and Goodhart (1992a) stress this point.

Three, and the national central banks could shift to the ECU too. Commercial banks would have to move in tandem with them in respect of their transactions with the central banks and one another, but not their transactions with the general public. These arrangements are illustrated in Chapter III.

The Constitution of the ESCB

The first draft of the ESCB Statute was prepared by the Committee of Central Bank Governors, whose members had served on the Delors Committee. The principal participants in the IGC on EMU came from Ministries of Finance and had rather different interests and concerns, yet the draft submitted to the Maastricht Summit was remarkably similar to the Governors Draft. The main differences are noted in due course below.[13]

The Mandate of the ESCB

The mandate of the ESCB is set out clearly in Article 2 of the Statute. It shall have as its "primary objective" the maintenance of price stability. Without prejudice to that objective, however, the ESCB "shall support the general economic policies in the Community" to contribute to the realization of the Community's objectives, laid down in the Treaty.[14] These include:

> ...balanced development of economic activities, sustainable and non-inflationary growth respecting the environment, a high degree of convergence of economic performance, a high level of employment and of social protection, the raising of the standard of living and quality of life, and economic and social cohesion [Article 2 of the Treaty].

These objectives may seem trite but should not be taken lightly. Because they are cited explicitly at the start of the Statute, the ESCB cannot ignore them. It must pay attention to employment, growth, and other goals whenever it can do so without jeopardizing price stability. Finally, the ESCB shall "act in accordance with the principle of an open market economy with free competition, favouring an efficient allocation of resources" [Article 2 of the Statute].

---

[13] Portions of the ESCB Statute are replicated in Articles 105-108 of the Treaty; for brevity, however, I cite the Statute here without also citing the Treaty. (All such references in this section pertain to the ESCB Statute, not the EMI Statute.) Elsewhere in this monograph, I follow common practice and refer to the ECB when discussing monetary policy in Stage Three. In the rest of this chapter, however, I follow the Statute and refer to the ESCB whenever the Statute does so.

[14] There is a small but important difference between this phrasing and that of the governors, who referred to the economic policy "of" the Community. Apparently, "of" was seen to invite the ESCB to disregard the policies of the individual EC countries and seemed also to invite the Community to adopt a wide range of common policies. The invitation to set common policies was even stronger in the Delors Report (1989), which said that the ESCB should "support the general economic policies set at the Community level" and recommended that the Community develop such policies and set guidelines for national policies; see the quotations in Chapter I above and the section on coordinating national policies in Chapter IV below.

The tasks of the ESCB are set out in Article 3 of the Statute:

- to define and implement the monetary policy of the Community;
- to conduct foreign exchange operations consistent with the provisions of Article 109 of this Treaty;
- to hold and manage the official foreign reserves of the Member States;
- to promote the smooth operation of payment systems.

In addition, the ESCB "shall contribute to the smooth conduct of policies pursued by the competent authorities relating to the prudential supervision of credit institutions and the stability of the financial system."

There are two important differences between this list and the one in the Governors Draft—one half hidden and the other all too clear.

First, Article 109 of the Treaty, pertaining to exchange-rate policy and discussed in the next section of this chapter, contains provisions different from those the governors contemplated when they prepared their draft. Under certain circumstances, the ESCB might be compelled to intervene on foreign-exchange markets even when such intervention would be inconsistent with the maintenance of price stability.

Second, the Governors Draft gave the ESCB much more to say and do about prudential supervision. It would "participate as necessary in the formulation, co-ordination and execution of policies relating to prudential supervision and the stability of the financial system." It would not merely "contribute to the smooth functioning" of policies designed and pursued by others. The Governors Draft also said that the ECB would be "entitled to offer advice and to be consulted" on the interpretation and implementation of Community legislation relating to prudential supervision and would "formulate, interpret and implement policies relating to the prudential supervision of credit and other financial institutions for which it is designated as competent supervisory authority."

But the governors left to the IGC the method by which the ECB would be so designated, and it decided to make this difficult. In fact, it weakened the Governors Draft in two vital ways. Under Article 25 of the Statute, the ECB "may" offer advice and be consulted—which is much weaker than the governors' "is entitled to". And under Article 105 of the Treaty,

> ...the Council may, acting unanimously on a proposal from the Commission and after consulting the ECB and after receiving the assent of the European Parliament, confer upon the ECB specific tasks concerning policies relating to the prudential supervision of credit institutions and other financial institutions with the exception of insurance undertakings.

No one could have built a higher set of hurdles.[15]

---

[15] The reduction of the role of the ECB in prudential matters took place late in the IGC. In the Netherlands Draft, six weeks before Maastricht, the wording of Article 25 was closer to the governors' wording than to the final version. Furthermore, the hurdles in the Treaty were fewer and lower; the Council was to act by qualified majority, not unanimity, and the assent of the Parliament was not required.

The Community's Second Banking Directive creates a single market for banking services; the banks of every EC country will be free to establish subsidiaries or branches in all other EC countries. Under the principle of "mutual recognition," they will be subject to home-country (consolidated) supervision but will have to conform to common capital-adequacy standards.[16]

These rules, however, may be inadequate:

Europe starts from a position of having quite different forms of bank regulation across countries. In some countries there are limitations on bank equity holdings and the form of bank loans and specific liquidity requirements. Some countries provide quite generous deposit insurance; others do not. In some countries, central banks undertake bank supervision themselves; in others, it is contracted out to auditors.

In a system of segmented financial markets, differences in bank regulation can be tolerated; in integrated markets they cannot. There are four important "externalities" that cause investors in one country to be affected by regulation in others.

First, not all customers of banks are domestic residents. Some of the effects of financial failure are felt by depositors overseas...or by those who are required to pay deposit insurance.

Second, failure may not be restricted to individual banks, and the failure of one bank may cast doubt on the ability of other banks in a country to survive...

Third, a failure in one country could spread contagiously across Europe as well as within countries. More seriously, as markets become integrated, the exposure of banks in one country to those in another increases. This may result...through the interbank market, which will become much more integrated even before the emergence of a single currency...

Fourth, with the emergence of the single European currency, banking failures may have repercussions...through the payments system.... In determining the extent to which lender of last resort facilities should be provided, account must be taken of the Community-wide consequences of interruptions to payments.

Externalities involving the operation of the payments system and the interbank market therefore mean that decisions cannot be left to national regulators. ... Decisions concerning the authorization and rescuing of banks need to be coordinated at a European level, whereas principles of subsidiarity allow them to be taken at a lower level for other financial institutions.[17]

---

[16] These standards were adopted by Basle Committee on Banking Supervision under the auspices of the Bank for International Settlements (BIS); they will come into force in 1993 and will apply to Canadian, Japanese, and US banks as well as EC banks. They are embodied with minor modifications in EC Directives.

[17] Chiappori et al. (1991), pp. 72-74. Their paper goes on to describe the cross-country differences in regulation and deposit-insurance arrangements and makes comprehensive proposals for EC-wide regulation. While I agree with their statement of the problem and their main recommendations, I have doubts about their organizational proposals. They argue that the

These considerations do not necessarily mean that the ECB should take over prudential supervision. That responsibility is divided in a number of European countries, including France and Germany. But the ECB must be involved, not only as a lender of last resort, but also in closing or restructuring banks.

Why the ECB? Why not the national central banks? They can and must be involved—and some will continue to supervise their own countries' banks in Stage Three. But serious conflicts could arise if one of the national central banks were to act as lender of last resort to credit institutions having severe liquidity problems, and its lending were seen by the ECB as threatening the stance of monetary policy.

Begg et al. (1991) discount this possibility, because they believe that lending to distressed institutions can be offset completely by open-market operations and thus need not interfere with price stability. But Chiappori et al. (1991) take a grimmer view, as do Folkerts-Landau and Garber (1991), who argue that highly developed financial systems are very vulnerable to liquidity crises and that these can disrupt the entire payments system or lead to large price changes on financial markets. To serve as lenders of last resort in these circumstances, central banks may have to operate aggressively in ways that cannot be offset by open-market operations. In fact, they may have to *use* open-market operations to make enough credit available. Folkerts-Landau and Garber cite the 1987 stock market crash; it would have been much worse, they say, in the absence of massive intervention by the Federal Reserve, which permitted dealers and others to repay their call loans without selling more securities and driving down stock prices further.[18]

If the problem of systemic stability looms larger in the 1990s and the problem of inflation recedes, the language of the ESCB Statute may prove to be anachronistic even before it takes effect.[19]

---

agency which licenses banks should not be involved in decisions to restructure or close them, as it may be reluctant to admit mistakes. Hence, licensing and lender-of-last-resort operations should be assigned to the ESCB, but supervision, deposit insurance, and closure should be assigned to another agency (or agencies). This proposal, however, is open to the authors' own objection. Supervisors may not want to admit mistakes, and the agency responsible for deposit insurance may not want to restructure or close a bank because of the cost to the insurance fund. Furthermore, a closure can have serious effects on other institutions unless it is carefully managed; that was shown clearly in the Bankhaus Herstatt case of 1974. Therefore, central banks must be involved in decisions about closures and in their implementation. Note that the four "externalities" listed in the text argued for more coordination at a global level—or something even more ambitious—not merely within Europe.

[18] See also Folkerts-Landau (1991).

[19] One must nevertheless concede the validity of the objection made by a close observer of the EMU negotiations. Had the ECB been charged with pursuing financial stability as well as price stability, it might not have won as much independence; governments might have felt that too much was at stake.

The Organization of the ESCB

The European System of Central Banks (ESCB) will consist of the national central banks and the European Central Bank (ECB). It will be governed by the decision-making bodies of the ECB, as shown in Figure 4. The national central banks will be the only shareholders in the ECB, and their subscriptions to its capital will depend on a key whose weights will depend on the shares of their countries in the total population of the EC and their shares in its total GNP.[20]

The ECB will have an Executive Board and a Governing Council.[21] As was indicated earlier, the Executive Board will have a president, vice-president, and four other members; they will be appointed by "common accord" of the heads of state or government for 8-year nonrenewable terms. The six members of the Executive Board will be voting members of the Governing Council, along with the governors of the national central banks. Apart from decisions on certain financial matters, which must be made by weighted voting, decisions by the Board and the Governing Council will be taken by simple majority voting, with the president able to cast a tie-breaking vote.

The responsibilities of the two decision-making bodies are defined by Article 12 of the Statute, which reads in part:

> The Governing Council shall adopt the guidelines and take the decisions necessary to ensure the performance of the tasks entrusted to the ESCB under this Treaty and this Statute. The Governing Council shall formulate the monetary policy of the Community including, as appropriate, decisions relating to intermediate monetary objectives, key interest rates and the supply of reserves in the ESCB, and shall establish the necessary guidelines for their implementation.

> The Executive Board shall implement monetary policy in accordance with the guidelines and decisions laid down by the Governing Council. In doing so the Executive Board shall give the necessary instructions to national central banks. In addition the Executive Board may have certain powers delegated to it where the Governing Council so decides.

> To the extent deemed possible and appropriate and without prejudice to the provisions of this Article, the ECB shall have recourse to the national central banks to carry out operations which form part of the tasks of the ESCB.

In addition, the Board will prepare the meetings of the Governing Council, while the Governing Council will adopt the internal rules of the ECB and exercise its advisory functions vis-à-vis other Community bodies.

---

[20] Articles 28, 29, 32, and 33 of the Statute deal with the capital, key, and disposition of the income of the ECB and of the national central banks. The rest of this sub-section draws mainly on Articles 8 through 14 of the Statute (but does not touch on every matter covered by them).

[21] If some countries do not participate in Stage Three, a third body, the General Council, will be established; it will include the president and vice-president of the ECB and the governors of all twelve EC central banks. Its role is discussed in Chapter VI.

Note that the text is silent on one basic issue. Which body will decide when it is "possible and appropriate" for the ECB to "have recourse to" the national central banks? Will this be done by the Governing Council, by way of adopting the "guidelines" for implementing monetary policy? Or will it be done by the Board, by way of giving "instructions" to the national central banks? This matter will come up again in Chapter III.

The national central banks are deemed to be "an integral part of the ESCB" and must follow guidelines and instructions from the ECB. Nevertheless, they may perform functions other than those specified in the Statute, unless the Governing Council finds, by a two-thirds vote, that these interfere with the work of the ESCB.

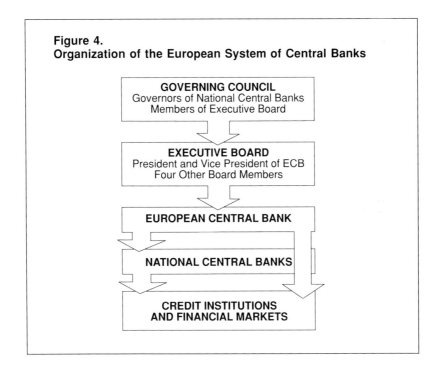

Figure 4.
Organization of the European System of Central Banks

GOVERNING COUNCIL
Governors of National Central Banks
Members of Executive Board

EXECUTIVE BOARD
President and Vice President of ECB
Four Other Board Members

EUROPEAN CENTRAL BANK

NATIONAL CENTRAL BANKS

CREDIT INSTITUTIONS
AND FINANCIAL MARKETS

The Powers of the ESCB
Although the ECB must make use of the national central banks whenever "possible and appropriate," it may conduct open-market and credit operations for its own account. Furthermore, the ESCB as a whole has wide powers in the monetary field.[22]

---

[22] Its duties and powers in the international field are examined in the next section of this chapter. This sub-section draws on Articles 16 through 22 of the Statute.

The Governing Council will have the exclusive right to authorize the issue of bank notes in the ESCB countries, although the notes themselves may be issued by the ECB or by the national central banks. These will be the only notes to have legal-tender status in the ESCB countries.[23]

The ECB and national central banks may buy and sell securities and other claims, spot or forward, outright or for repurchase, and in EC or foreign currencies, and it may borrow and lend securities; it may also operate in precious metals. There are no restrictions whatsoever on eligibility. The ECB and national central banks can also conduct credit operations with banks and other institutions, but lending must be based on adequate collateral.[24] The ECB is required to establish "general principles" for open-market and credit operations and to announce the conditions under which the ECB and national central banks stand ready to engage in them.

The ECB may require banks to hold minimum reserves in accounts with itself and the national central banks and to levy penalties for noncompliance. But the Council of Ministers has first to adopt enabling legislation defining the basis for holding those reserves (e.g., the deposit base), the highest permissible reserve ratio, and the appropriate penalties.

Finally, the Governing Council may decide by a two-thirds vote to use "other operational methods of monetary control" as it sees fit.

The ECB and national central banks may act as fiscal agents for public entities but may not grant them credit facilities or buy debt instruments directly from them.[25] They may also provide facilities—and the ECB may issue regulations—to "ensure efficient and sound clearing and payment systems within the Community and with other countries."

The ESCB and the ECU Exchange Rate

The official reserves of EC countries include gold, EC currencies, other foreign currencies, ECU balances held with the EMCF, reserve positions in the International Monetary Fund (IMF), and Special Drawing Rights

---

[23] This provision raised problems for the United Kingdom, as Scottish banks issue bank notes of their own. Therefore another sentence was added to Article 16 of the Statute: "The ECB shall respect as far as possible existing practices regarding the issue and design of bank notes." Under Article 105a of the Treaty, national governments may issue coins in amounts subject to ECB approval, but the Community is entitled to adopt legislation standardizing denominations and technical specifications. Queen Beatrix of the Netherlands made a gracious concession to the success of EMU at the Maastricht Summit. "On my part," she said, "I assure you that I am prepared to make a contribution by sacrificing my head on our coinage to the ECU."

[24] The collateral requirement calls into question the ability of the ECB to act as lender of last resort. Credit institutions able to put up adequate collateral can usually borrow commercially—unless financial markets are hit by a systemic crisis. The institutions needing central-bank credit are those that might have trouble providing collateral.

[25] This prohibition also appears as Article 104 of the Treaty and is discussed in the last section of this chapter. Goodhart (1992a) points out that Article 104 may force governments to replace

(SDRs) issued by the IMF. By the start of Stage Three, reserve assets held by participating governments must be shifted to their central banks, and the central banks, in turn, must transfer some of their reserves to the ECB.[26] The use of reserves retained by the national central banks may be regulated by the ECB to ensure consistency with the exchange-rate and monetary policies of the Community.

But the powers of the ECB are likewise limited, because Article 109 of the Treaty divides responsibility for exchange-rate policy between the Council of Ministers and the ECB. The full text will be found in Chapter VI, where it will figure importantly in the discussion of policy coordination and exchange-rate management at the global level. But its principal provisions can be summarized briefly:

- Acting unanimously, the Council may conclude agreements on an exchange-rate system for the ECU in relation to non-Community currencies. It must consult the ECB in an effort to achieve a "consensus" consistent with price stability, but once the Council has acted, the agreements will be binding on the ECB, which must implement them even if they interfere with price stability.

- Acting by qualified majority, the Council may adopt "general orientations" for exchange-rate policy relative to non-Community currencies. But these broad guidelines must not conflict with price stability.

The Treaty does not indicate, however, who will decide whether the "general orientations" conflict with price stability. (It was suggested at one point that the European Court of Justice be asked to rule on the question, which is a bit like asking the US Supreme Court to decide when a foetus is viable. As the analogy suggests, however, strange things do happen. Fortunately, this proposal was dropped.)

Until the Council of Ministers takes one of these two steps, the ECB is apparently free to decide whether to intervene on foreign-exchange markets, unilaterally or in concert with foreign central banks. Once the Council has acted, however, the autonomy of the ECB will be circumscribed,

---

their central-bank credit lines with commercial-bank credit lines, and this may lead them to transfer other functions to private-sector institutions. Hence, the national central banks may cease to function as fiscal agents for their governments.

[26] Governments can continue to hold working balances, and the reserve assets transferred to the ECB may not include EC currencies, ECU balances, IMF reserve positions, or SDRs, which are not easily used for intervention on the foreign-exchange markets. Nevertheless, the ECB is authorized to hold and manage IMF reserve positions and SDRs and to provide for the pooling of those assets. The initial transfer to the ECB may not exceed ECU 50 billion, and each central bank's share in the total will be proportional to its share in the capital of the ECB; see Article 30 of the Statute. (These arrangements suggest that the ECB is expected to conduct exchange-market intervention on its own and for its own account, with reserve assets supplied by the national central banks. The principle of subsidiarity, which calls on the ECB to use the national central banks for open-market and credit operations, is not invoked with regard to exchange-market operations.)

not only with regard to exchange-rate management but also in the conduct of monetary policy, because intervention on foreign-exchange markets can affect the money supply.

Independence and Accountability

Several provisions in the Treaty and Statute bear on the independence of the ECB. The most important is Article 107 of the Treaty,[27] which applies to the ECB and the national central banks:

> When exercising the powers and carrying out the tasks and duties conferred upon them by this Treaty and the Statute of the ESCB, neither the ECB, nor a national central bank, nor any member of their decision-making bodies shall seek or take instructions from Community institutions or bodies, from any Government of a Member State or from any other body. The Community institutions and bodies and the governments of the Member States undertake to respect this principle and not to seek to influence the members of the decision-making bodies of the ECB or of the national central banks in the performance of their tasks.

This injunction is reinforced by the prohibition cited earlier. As members of the Executive Board cannot be reappointed, they will have no incentive to please politicians—not those of member states or those of the Community.[28] Under Article 14 of the Statute, moreover, the term of office of a central bank governor can be no shorter than 5 years (though reappointment is not ruled out). Other articles protect the Executive Board and governors of national central banks from being dismissed arbitrarily.[29]

But the president of the Council of Ministers and a member of the EC Commission may participate without vote in the Governing Council of the ECB, and the president of the Council may submit a motion for consideration by the Governing Council.[30]

The fiscal provisions of the Treaty, discussed in Chapter IV, are meant in large measure to protect the independence of the ESCB. But they may not be very effective from that point of view. Recall the rule cited

---

[27] It is reproduced in full as Article 7 of the Statute (and also appears with appropriate modifications as Article 8 of the EMI Statute).

[28] Eichengreen (1992a) points out, however, that Board members may try to please politicians precisely because their terms are nonrenewable; they will need new jobs after 8 years on the Board. For a thorough treatment of this issue and more references, see Neumann (1991).

[29] Under Article 108 of the Treaty, participating countries must make their national legislation compatible with these and other provisions of the Treaty and of the ESCB Statute before Stage Three begins. The French Finance Minister announced at Maastricht that France would do this quickly, but the Chancellor of the Exchequer has since said that the status of the Bank of England will not be altered unless and until Britain decides to participate in Stage Three.

[30] Article 109b of the Treaty, which also provides that the president of the ECB shall be invited to participate in meetings of the Council of Ministers whenever it discusses matters relating to the work of the ESCB.

above against the "monetary financing" of official entities. The ECB and national central banks may not grant them credit or buy securities directly from them. This prohibition will prevent any government from requiring the ECB and national central banks to print high-powered money. Suppose, however, that a large EC country runs a big fiscal deficit. Even if not "excessive" under the criteria discussed in Chapter IV, the deficit may be big enough to confront the ECB with a difficult problem, much like the one that the Federal Reserve System faced in the early 1980s, when the United States began to run large budget deficits. If the ECB does not alter its monetary policy, EC interest rates may rise, "crowding out" domestic investment, and an inflow of foreign capital may cause the ECU to appreciate on foreign-exchange markets, "crowding out" the domestic production of tradable goods. Hence, the ECB may have to engage in indirect "monetary financing" by intervening on domestic financial markets to keep interest rates from rising or intervening on foreign-exchange markets to keep the ECU from rising.[31]

In what ways will the ESCB be accountable for its actions? Although the proceedings of the Governing Board will be confidential, the ECB will publish a quarterly report on the activities of the ESCB and will make an annual report to the Council, Commission, European Council, and European Parliament. Furthermore, the president of the ECB will present the report to the Council and the Parliament, which may debate it. Finally, the president of the ECB and other members of the Board may be heard by the appropriate committees of the Parliament, at the request of the Parliament or on their own initiative.

In one basic sense, however, the ESCB will be more independent than any other central bank—even the Bundesbank—and thus less accountable.[32] The powers of the European Parliament vis-à-vis the ESCB are much smaller than those of the German Parliament vis-à-vis the Bundesbank or those of the US Congress vis-à-vis the Federal Reserve System. Those two legislatures can amend the laws defining the powers and duties of their central banks and can even abolish the central banks by rescinding the relevant laws. But the ESCB Statute is a protocol to the Treaty, and any amendment to the Treaty or its protocols must be ratified by all EC countries.[33]

---

[31] This point has made many times; see, e.g., Buiter and Kletzer (1990) and Giovannini and Spaventa (1991). The problem is not solved by forbidding the ECB to make open-market purchases of government securities, as proposed by Neumann (1991); the ECB could still buy private debt to keep interest rates from rising.

[32] This paragraph and the next draw on Kenen (1991a). They explain the statement in Chapter I that those who wanted to replace the Bundesbank with a European institution, responsive to the needs of the EC as a whole, may be disappointed by the outcome at Maastricht.

[33] Under Article 106 of the Treaty, some articles of the Statute may be amended by the Council, acting by a qualified majority on a recommendation from the ECB, after consulting the Commission and receiving the assent sf the Parliament. (Alternatively, it can act unanimously

Therefore, the ESCB will not be accountable in the same fundamental sense that the Bundesbank and Federal Reserve are accountable. Those who render an accounting should, presumably, conduct themselves in ways that earn the approval of those to whom they render the accounting. To make the ESCB truly accountable in this sense, the Community must do more to close the "democratic deficit" by giving the European Parliament the power to initiate and even to enact amendments to the ESCB Statute.[34]

---

on a proposal from the Commission, in which case it must consult the ECB and must still have the assent of the Parliament.) But the articles in question relate mainly to administrative and financial matters and the scope of ECB operations—the conduct of open-market and credit operations and the imposition of reserve requirements. The Council cannot alter the objectives or tasks of the ESCB, its constitution, or the provisions protecting its independence.

[34] Goodhart (1992a) gives another reason for saying that the ESCB will not be accountable. Price stability is not defined operationally in the Treaty or ESCB Statute, allowing the ESCB to say that it has done what was possible under the circumstances. He is right, but even if the Treaty or ESCB Statute provided an explicit definition and the ESCB fell short of achieving it, no one could do anything about it. Goodhart concedes this point and recommends the arrangement introduced in New Zealand, where the government has entered into a formal contract with the Governor of the Reserve Bank, under which the Governor's reappointment depends on achieving an explicit quantitative target. See also Neumann (1991).

III. Monetary Policy in Stage Three

This chapter is concerned with monetary mechanics in Stage Three of EMU and the conduct of monetary policy by the ECB. It concentrates on problems stemming from the use of national currencies early in Stage Three but looks at ways to hasten and facilitate the transition to the ECU.

The first part of the chapter seeks to identify some institutional adaptations that would help to underwrite the locking of exchange rates and integrate the banking systems of the ESCB countries into a unified monetary system. The analytical framework draws on the experience of the United States, where transactions between banks in different Federal Reserve Districts give rise to transactions between the Federal Reserve Banks themselves.

The second part of the chapter describes the present practices of EC central banks to show what changes might be needed in Stage Three of EMU. It also examines the targeting of monetary policy, asking if the ECB should focus entirely on managing interest rates or concern itself with monetary aggregates as well. It argues that aggregates matter and may matter more in Stage Three of EMU, as the ECB will have better control over the total money supply of the ESCB countries than the individual central banks have now over their own national money supplies.

The third part of the chapter asks how the ECB might make use of the national central banks to carry out its policies and whether the ECB should distribute its open-market operations among the securities issued by the various EC governments. It also examines the use of reserve requirements. They are not absolutely necessary for managing money effectively but are used by several EC central banks. They may be helpful to the ECB, especially if it concerns itself with managing the quantity of credit, not only with managing interest rates. But difficult questions will have to be answered.

Monetary Mechanics in a Federal System

Suppose that the following conditions obtain at the beginning of Stage Three, when the ECB has been established and the values of national currencies have been fixed irrevocably in terms of the ECU:

1. The balance sheets of the ECB and the national central banks are denominated in ECU.

2. Credit institutions hold ECU balances with their national central banks. They may or may not be *required* to hold them; the examples provided below are equally valid in both cases.[1]

3. There is an ECB Funds market, where credit institutions can make or take interbank loans and thus lend or borrow ECU cash balances held at the national central banks.

4. Governments have attached "ECU endorsements" to all of their marketable obligations, guaranteeing to redeem them in ECU, and similar endorsements are attached to all other instruments used in open-market operations.[2]

5. There is a unified market for all securities bearing ECU endorsements, where interest rates on individual issues differ only in so far as the issues themselves differ in default risk, liquidity, and taxability.

6. Firms and individuals still use their own national currencies but also hold and deal in securities with ECU endorsements.

The method of fixing of exchange rates will be discussed when the problem arises below.

The Balance Sheets of the Banking System

The schematic balance sheets in Figure 5 illustrate some of the consequences of these suppositions.[3] The ESCB is represented by the ECB, the Banque de France and the Bundesbank; French and German credit institutions are represented by the Banque Nationale de Paris and the Commerzbank; the private sectors are represented by "Jean" in France and "Karl" in Germany. Normally, Jean does business in francs, using the Banque Nationale de Paris, while Karl does business in marks, using the Commerzbank.

The liabilities of the central-banking institutions are denominated in ECU, but some of their assets are not. Their foreign-exchange reserves, of

---

[1] But the subsequent paths of the monetary aggregates will, of course, depend on the presence or absence of reserve requirements.

[2] These other instruments could be endorsed by the original issuers or by the institutions selling them to the ESCB.

[3] Certain items are omitted from these balance sheets, even though they appear on subsequent balance sheets illustrating the effects of particular transactions. Interbank deposits and loans, for instance, appear at various points in Example A, dealing with a payment from Jean to Karl.

course, are denominated in third-country currencies, and their holdings of securities are still denominated in francs and marks, although they bear ECU endorsements (EE). The deposit liabilities of the credit institutions are denominated in national currencies, but debts owed to the central banks are ECU-denominated. The assets of the credit institutions include ECU-denominated balances held at the central banks, securities denominated

---

Figure 5.
Schematic Balance Sheets at the
Beginning of Stage Three

European Central Bank

Assets	Liabilities
FF Securities (ECU endorsed) DM Securities (ECU endorsed) Foreign-Exchange Reserves	ECU Deposits owed to Banque de France and Bundesbank

Banque de France

Assets	Liabilities
ECU Deposit at European Central Bank FF Securities (ECU endorsed) ECU Credit Extended to Banque Nationale de Paris Foreign-Exchange Reserves	ECU Deposit owed to Banque Nationale de Paris

Bundesbank

Assets	Liabilities
ECU Deposit at European Central Bank DM Securities (ECU endorsed) ECU Credit Extended to Commerzbank Foreign-Exchange Reserves	ECU Deposit owed to Commerzbank

Banque Nationale de Paris

Assets	Liabilities
ECU Deposit at Banque de France FF Securities (ECU endorsed) FF Loans to Jean	FF Deposit owed to Jean ECU Credit Extended by Banque de France

Commerzbank

Assets	Liabilities
ECU Deposit at Bundesbank DM Securities (ECU endorsed) DM Loans to Karl	DM Deposit owed to Karl ECU Credit Extended by Bundesbank

in francs and marks but bearing ECU endorsements, and national-currency loans to Jean and Karl. When the ECU has replaced the national currencies, all of these items will be expressed in ECU, apart from foreign-exchange holdings. It is therefore easy to see that statements made below about transactions in national currencies will continue to hold later in Stage Three, after the switch to the ECU. (Some transactions may take fewer steps, however, depending on the ways in which cross-border payments are made and cleared.)

These schematic balance sheets can be used to examine the effects of cross-border transactions and of operations by the ESCB. Two examples are given here, a payment from Jean to Karl and an open-market purchase, with several permutations in each instance. More examples are given in an Appendix to this chapter. (Readers who wish to the skip the examples will find the conclusions on p. 45.)

A Payment from Jean to Karl
Suppose that Jean pays Karl the ECU equivalent of DM 100. The effects are shown at Step 1 of Example A. (In this and other examples, the start of the current step is marked by an arrow in the corresponding figure.) Jean will acquire the marks in the usual way—by drawing on his account at the Banque Nationale de Paris, which will draw a check on its working balance with the Commerzbank. When Karl receives the check from Jean, he will deposit it at the Commerzbank, which will debit the account of the Banque Nationale de Paris. But how will the Banque Nationale de Paris reconstitute its working balance? That is where the fixing of exchange rates starts to matter. Before Stage Three, the Banque Nationale de Paris would have bought marks with francs in the foreign-exchange market, paying the market-determined exchange rate. At the start of Stage Three, however,

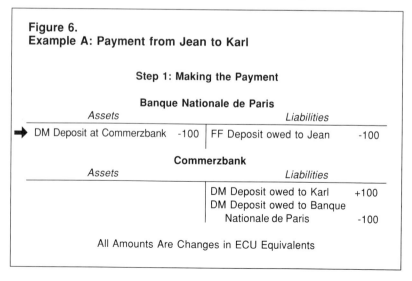

Figure 6.
Example A: Payment from Jean to Karl

Step 1: Making the Payment

Banque Nationale de Paris

Assets		Liabilities	
➡ DM Deposit at Commerzbank	-100	FF Deposit owed to Jean	-100

Commerzbank

Assets		Liabilities	
		DM Deposit owed to Karl	+100
		DM Deposit owed to Banque Nationale de Paris	-100

All Amounts Are Changes in ECU Equivalents

36

the market-determined rate will be replaced by an exchange rate fixed exactly at the cross rate given by the ECU values of the franc and mark, and the central banks will be obliged to keep that rate from changing. They could do this in the ordinary way—by intervening in the interbank market. They could also do it, however, by swapping their own currencies for ECU (or for the currencies of other ESCB countries when banks need those currencies).

This approach is illustrated at Step 2 of Example A, which reverses the initial change in the balance of the Banque Nationale de Paris at the

---

Figure 7.
Example A: Payment from Jean to Karl

Step 2: Clearing the Payment

European Central Bank

Assets	Liabilities	
	ECU Deposit owed to Banque de France	-100
	ECU Deposit owed to Bundesbank	+100

Banque de France

Assets		Liabilities	
ECU Deposit at European Central Bank	-100	ECU Deposit owed to Banque Nationale de Paris	-100

Bundesbank

Assets		Liabilities	
ECU Deposit at European Central Bank	+100	ECU Deposit owed to Commerzbank	+100

Banque Nationale de Paris

Assets		Liabilities	
DM Deposit at Commerzbank -100		FF Deposit owed to Jean	-100
➡ ECU Deposit at Banque de France	-100		

Commerzbank

Assets	Liabilities	
ECU Deposit at Bundesbank +100	DM Deposit owed to Karl	+100
	DM Deposit owed to Banque Nationale de Paris	-100

All Amounts Are Changes in ECU Equivalents
Shaded Entries Are Reversals of Previous Entries

Commerzbank. (Reversals of earlier changes are shown by shading the affected items rather than deleting them). To rebuild its balance at the Commerzbank, the Banque Nationale de Paris would buy ECU (or marks) from the Banque de France by drawing down its balance there and would deposit them with the Commerzbank; the Commerzbank would deposit the ECU with the Bundesbank; and the transaction would be completed by transfers on the books of the ECB. The Banque de France would draw down its balance at the ECB to obtain the ECU needed by the Banque Nationale de Paris, and the Bundesbank would deposit at the ECB the ECU obtained from the Commerzbank.

The steps illustrated by Step 2 look to be cumbersome. But they are not needed every time French and German residents deal with each other. They take place only when the *sum* of the transactions leads to a net change in the working balances of French or German banks.[4] The central banks get involved in clearing transactions only when the dealings between French and German residents would have led to an imbalance in the foreign-exchange market had exchange rates not been locked. In other words, the entries for the Banque de France, Bundesbank, and ECB resemble those that would occur with nonsterilized intervention in the foreign-exchange market. One must not carry this analogy too far, however, as the entries on the books of the Banque de France and Bundesbank do not call for changes in their monetary policies. There can be no such changes in a monetary union—and we will soon see how the entries are reversed.

One other observation should be made before taking that next step. The entries shown at Step 2 are not peculiar to the use of national currencies by Jean and Karl. When the ECU replaces those currencies, Jean can pay Karl by writing a check on his ECU-denominated balance at the Banque Nationale de Paris; he will not have to buy marks from the Banque Nationale de Paris. But the entries required to clear his check will resemble the entries at Step 2 required to reconstitute the working balance of the Banque Nationale de Paris. (This same statement holds for all the examples below. They use national currencies to show that they apply from the start of Stage Three, but use of the ECU would not alter them importantly.)

Reserve requirements might matter at the end of Step 2, as the Banque Nationale de Paris has lost reserves and the Commerzbank has gained them. Even if there were reserve requirements, however, and they were binding, there might be no further effect on lending or monetary aggregates. There are two ways in which the Banque Nationale de Paris can acquire reserves from the Commerzbank:

- It can borrow reserves from the Commerzbank in the ECB Funds market, with the results shown at Step 3a of Example A. The loan appears on the liability side of the Banque Nationale de Paris balance

---

[4] If both countries' banks experience reductions in their working balances, they can rebuild them by crediting each other, without involving the central banks.

sheet, and the clearing of that loan through the central banks reverses all of the Step 2 entries on the books of the central-banking system.[5]
- It can sell FF securities having ECU endorsements, and the Commerzbank can buy them, with the results shown at Step 3b. The clearing of payments for the securities reverses the Step Two entries.[6]

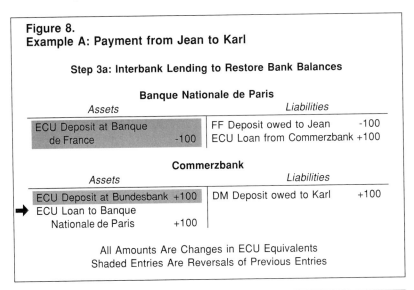

Figure 8.
Example A: Payment from Jean to Karl

Step 3a: Interbank Lending to Restore Bank Balances

Banque Nationale de Paris

Assets		Liabilities	
ECU Deposit at Banque de France	-100	FF Deposit owed to Jean	-100
		ECU Loan from Commerzbank	+100

Commerzbank

Assets		Liabilities	
ECU Deposit at Bundesbank	+100	DM Deposit owed to Karl	+100
ECU Loan to Banque Nationale de Paris	+100		

All Amounts Are Changes in ECU Equivalents
Shaded Entries Are Reversals of Previous Entries

Figure 9.
Example A: Payment from Jean to Karl

Step 3b: Transactions in Securities to Restore Bank Balances

Banque Nationale de Paris

Assets		Liabilities	
ECU Deposit at Banque de France	-100	FF Deposit owed to Jean	-100
FF Securities (ECU endorsed)	-100		

Commerzbank

Assets		Liabilities	
ECU Deposit at Bundesbank	+100	DM Deposit owed to Karl	+100
FF Securities (ECU endorsed)	+100		

All Amounts Are Changes in ECU Equivalents
Shaded Entries Are Reversals of Previous Entries

---

5 The central banks' balance sheets are not shown at Steps 3a and 3b, as the relevant entries would merely cancel (shade) the entries shown at Step 2.

6 If the Commerzbank wanted to buy DM securities, not FF securities, the sale by the Banque Nationale de Paris would tend to raise interest rates on FF securities, the purchase by the Commerzbank would tend to reduce interest rates on DM securities, and the two banks would

Another important possibility has to be illustrated. If the Step 2 entries are not reversed in one of the ways described above, the Banque de France will have run down its balance with the ECB and the Bundesbank will have built up its balance. Step 4 shows how these changes could be offset. (It omits the balance sheets of the Banque Nationale de Paris and Commerzbank, which stay as they were at the end of Step 2.) The ECB could "buy" bonds from the Banque de France and "sell" bonds to the Bundesbank. In effect, the balance sheet of the ECB would play the role of the Interdistrict Settlement Fund in the Federal Reserve System, which transfers US Government securities among the Federal Reserve Banks to balance their accounts with each other. These transactions do not affect monetary conditions in France or Germany, and the central banks need not reverse them in the future. They are mere bookkeeping transfers within the central-banking system, not forms of liquidity or balance-of-payments support like those provided in the EMS. They would in fact vanish completely from a consolidated balance sheet for the ESCB. That is why one must be so cautious about drawing analogies between central bank

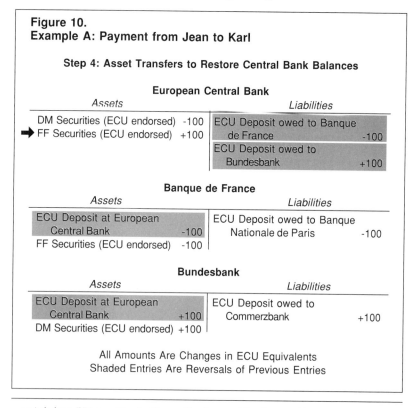

Figure 10.
Example A: Payment from Jean to Karl

Step 4: Asset Transfers to Restore Central Bank Balances

European Central Bank

Assets		Liabilities	
DM Securities (ECU endorsed)	-100	ECU Deposit owed to Banque de France	-100
➡ FF Securities (ECU endorsed)	+100	ECU Deposit owed to Bundesbank	+100

Banque de France

Assets		Liabilities	
ECU Deposit at European Central Bank	-100	ECU Deposit owed to Banque Nationale de Paris	-100
FF Securities (ECU endorsed)	-100		

Bundesbank

Assets		Liabilities	
ECU Deposit at European Central Bank	+100	ECU Deposit owed to Commerzbank	+100
DM Securities (ECU endorsed)	+100		

All Amounts Are Changes in ECU Equivalents
Shaded Entries Are Reversals of Previous Entries

switch from DM securities to FF securities in quantities that would cancel the interest-rate changes. The Banque Nationale de Paris balance sheet would show net sales of FF and DM securities, and the Commerzbank balance sheet would show net purchases of both securities.

transactions in a monetary union and seemingly similar reserve movements between independent central banks.[7]

An Open-Market Operation

Suppose that the ECB decides upon an open-market purchase of government or other eligible paper bearing an ECU endorsement and instructs the Banque de France to execute the purchase for its own account. Suppose further that the Banque Nationale de Paris is the seller of the bonds—whether because the Banque de France deals only with French banks or because the Banque Nationale de Paris makes the most competitive offer.[8]

The initial effects of the open-market purchase are shown at Step 1 of Example B. (The balance sheets of the ECB, the Bundesbank, and Commerzbank are omitted, as they are not affected at this stage.) The Banque Nationale de Paris holds fewer securities but more reserves at the Banque de France. The money supply does not change.[9] In the normal course of events, the Banque Nationale de Paris can be expected to lend out the increase in its liquid assets. If it lends to Jean, the results are straightforward, and they need not be shown separately. There will be the

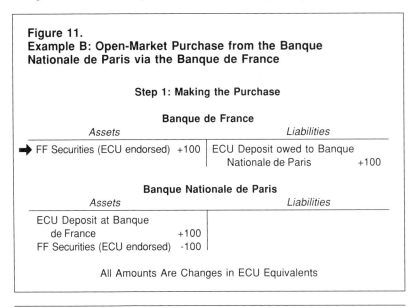

Figure 11.
Example B: Open-Market Purchase from the Banque Nationale de Paris via the Banque de France

Step 1: Making the Purchase

Banque de France

Assets	Liabilities
➡ FF Securities (ECU endorsed) +100	ECU Deposit owed to Banque Nationale de Paris +100

Banque Nationale de Paris

Assets	Liabilities
ECU Deposit at Banque de France +100 FF Securities (ECU endorsed) -100	

All Amounts Are Changes in ECU Equivalents

---

7   This point will come up again, when we come to the suggestion that the central banks' balances with the ECB might be used to regulate open-market and other credit operations in a system under which those operations would be initiated by the national central banks, not the ECB.

8   These possibilities and their implications are explored in the next part of this chapter (which also looks at other ways in which the ECB might conduct its open-market operations).

9   If Jean had sold the bonds, rather than the Banque Nationale de Paris, it would have risen by the ECU equivalent of FF 100. The Banque Nationale de Paris' balance sheet would have shown no change in holdings of securities, but the increase in its ECU deposit at the Banque de France would have been matched by an increase in the deposit owed to Jean.

Figure 12.
**Example B: Open-Market Purchase from the Banque
Nationale de Paris via the Banque de France**

Step 2: Lending the Proceeds to Karl

European Central Bank

Assets	Liabilities	
	ECU Deposits owed to Banque de France	-100
	ECU Deposit owed to Bundesbank	+100

Banque de France

Assets		Liabilities	
FF Securities (ECU endorsed)	+100	ECU Deposits owed to Banque Nationale de Paris	+100
ECU Deposit at European Central Bank	-100		

Bundesbank

Assets		Liabilities	
ECU Deposit at European Central Bank	+100	ECU Deposit owed to Commerzbank	+100

Banque Nationale de Paris

Assets		Liabilities
ECU Deposit at Banque de France	+100	
FF Securities (ECU endorsed)	-100	
➡ FF Loan to Karl	+100	

Commerzbank

Assets		Liabilities	
ECU Deposit at Bundesbank	+100	DM Deposit owed to Karl	+100

All Amounts Are Changes in ECU Equivalents
Shaded Entries Are Reversals of Previous Entries

usual cumulative increase in loans and deposits at French banks, with the size of the increase limited by the "leakage" of liquidity into currency holdings and, with reserve requirements, by the transfer of liquidity from "excess" to "required" reserves because of the increase in deposits at French banks.[10]

But let's look at another possibility. Suppose that the Banque Nationale de Paris lends to Karl, who is willing to incur franc-denominated debt but

---

[10] But some of the increase in lending and deposits might take place on the books of German banks, because borrowers from French banks might use some of the loan proceeds to make payments to Germany and thus transfer some of the increase in liquidity from French to German banks.

wants to transfer the loan proceeds to his mark-denominated account at the Commerzbank. The results are shown at Step 2 of Example B. The loan appears on its balance sheet, replacing the increase in the Banque Nationale de Paris' ECU deposit at the Banque de France. The loan *proceeds* appear on the Commerzbank's balance sheet, as an increase of DM deposits owed to Karl, and this entry increases the Commerzbank's ECU deposit at the Bundesbank. Finally, the transfer between the two banks gives rise to transfers on the books of the Banque de France, the Bundesbank, and the ECB. Similar results obtain, of course, when the Banque Nationale de Paris does not lend to Karl directly but makes an ECB Funds loan to the Commerzbank, which makes the loan to Karl.

What happens when the Commerzbank supplies the securities bought by the Banque de France? The results are illustrated by Example C. The changes in the Commerzbank's balance sheet resemble the changes in the Banque Nationale de Paris' balance sheet shown at Step 1a. The Commerzbank holds its cash balance at the Bundesbank, however, not at the Banque de France, which means that entries must be made on the books of the

---

Figure 13.
Example C: Open-Market Purchase from the Commerzbank via the Banque de France

European Central Bank

Assets	Liabilities	
	ECU Deposits owed to Banque de France	-100
	ECU Deposit owed to Bundesbank	+100

Banque de France

Assets		Liabilities
FF Securities (ECU endorsed)	+100	
ECU Deposit at European Central Bank	-100	

Bundesbank

Assets		Liabilities	
ECU Deposit at European Central Bank	+100	ECU Deposit owed to Commerzbank	+100

Commerzbank

Assets		Liabilities
ECU Deposit at Bundesbank	+100	
FF Securities (ECU endorsed)	-100	

All Amounts Are Changes in ECU Equivalents

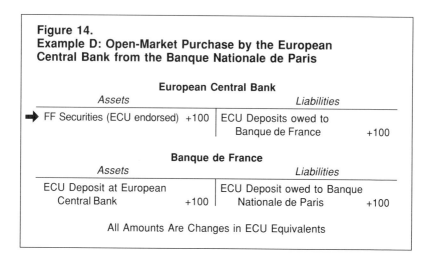

Figure 14.
Example D: Open-Market Purchase by the European
Central Bank from the Banque Nationale de Paris

European Central Bank

Assets	Liabilities
➡ FF Securities (ECU endorsed) +100	ECU Deposits owed to Banque de France +100

Banque de France

Assets	Liabilities
ECU Deposit at European Central Bank +100	ECU Deposit owed to Banque Nationale de Paris +100

All Amounts Are Changes in ECU Equivalents

Bundesbank and ECB to transfer the newly created cash from the Banque de France to the Bundesbank. (The entries are the same as those at Step 2 of Example A, where Jean's payment to Karl cleared through the ECB.)

What happens when the ECB makes the open-market purchase for its own account, instead of using a national central bank? The outcome depends mainly on the nationality of the other party to the transaction. If the Banque Nationale de Paris supplies the securities bought by the ECB, the entries on its balance sheet will look like those shown at Step 1 of Example B, but the entries on the central banks' balance sheets will be slightly different. They appear in Example D, where the open-market purchase appears on the books of the ECB, and the entries on the books of the Banque de France link that purchase with the entries on the books of the Banque Nationale de Paris. If the Commerzbank supplies the securities, the entries on its books will look like those in Example C, and the corresponding entries on the central banks' books will resemble those in Example D (but the Bundesbank will replace the Banque de France when the Commerzbank replaces the Banque Nationale de Paris). In both cases, of course, the ECB's balance sheet serves as something more than a settlement fund. It becomes the source of central-bank credit, which passes through the books of the national central banks on the way to its ultimate destination. But its route depends on its destination, which depends on the institution or individual making the sale to the ECB.

More transactions are examined in the Appendix to this chapter. They show how the ECB might intervene on foreign-exchange markets and how the central-banking system might cope with speculation caused by doubts about the irrevocability of the fixed exchange rates. But those additional examples merely reinforce the conclusions one can draw from the examples examined here:

- Cross-border settlements early in Stage Three, when national currencies are still used, will not differ greatly from those later in Stage Three, when the ECU has replaced the national currencies.
- The distributional effects of open-market operations depend on the identities of the counterparties, not of the central bank undertaking the operations.
- But an ECB Funds and integrated bond market will greatly reduce and may even neutralize the distributional effects of cross-border transactions and open-market operations.
- If the ECB does not operate in the securities or currency markets, but delegates those tasks to the national central banks, its balance sheet will play a role analogous to that of the Interdistrict Settlement Fund in the Federal Reserve System.
- Even when credit institutions are unwilling or unable to redistribute liquidity created by the ESCB, its distribution can affect the final users of bank credit only if they are unwilling or unable to engage in cross-border borrowing.

It is worth stressing, however, that some of these conclusions require the early development of an ECB Funds market and integrated market for national debt instruments.[11] To speed the development of those key markets, the ESCB should keep its books in ECU from the start of Stage Three, and national governments should redenominate or endorse their debts in ECU.

Techniques of Monetary Management in Europe

The ECB is expected to use the national central banks whenever "possible and appropriate" to implement its monetary policy. There are various ways to do that, involving different degrees of centralization, and some of them are examined later in this chapter. Most of them will force the national central banks to pursue the same targets and use similar techniques to conduct open-market and credit operations. Will they have to change their present practices extensively?

Interest Rates and Monetary Aggregates
A decade ago, the major EC central banks were pursuing rather strict quantitative targets defined in terms of growth rates for monetary aggregates. Different aggregates were used in different countries, and several countries shifted from one to another. Some EC central banks still publish and pursue targets of this sort. With the possible exception of the Bundesbank, however, they appear to attach less importance to them. The reasons are

---

[11] The ESCB banking system needs *both* markets to function effectively; they are not perfect substitutes, because borrowed and owned reserves are not perfect substitutes.

45

well known. The relationships between economic activity and the various monetary aggregates have not been sufficiently stable to justify relying on quantitative targets to regulate the conduct of monetary policy.

Financial innovation is frequently blamed for loosening the link between the money stock and level of activity, but it was not the only cause. Artis (1991), for example, shows that there has been somewhat more stability than might have been expected in the US and UK cases, although financial innovation was extensive in those countries, and somewhat less stability than might have expected in the German case, where innovation was less extensive.

Other explanations for the looser link focus on the endogeneity of money. When exchange rates are pegged, as in the ERM, the money supply can be affected strongly by official intervention on the foreign-exchange market and by changes in the foreign claims and liabilities of the banking system.[12] Furthermore, measures of the money stock commonly omit nonresidents' deposits with domestic banks and residents' deposits with foreign banks in domestic and foreign currencies alike. Corrections for these omissions have been shown to improve econometric estimates of the demand for money in some EC countries; see Angeloni, Cottarelli, and Levy (1991).

Whatever the reasons for the recent weakness of the link, the loss of confidence in monetary targeting has led EC central banks to emphasize the influence of interest rates on aggregate demand. Monetary aggregates, they say, continue to provide timely information about the behavior of aggregate demand, because monetary data are available more speedily than price or output data. When it comes to affecting aggregate demand, however, interest rates are now the instruments of choice, even in countries that do not have much freedom to set their own interest rates because they have to follow German rates.[13]

Interest rates matter. That much is clear. Furthermore, Artis (1991) shows that interest-rate effects did not weaken in the 1980s. The current emphasis on interest rates, however, raises an old question. Is there any significant difference between a policy that seeks to influence the cost of

---

[12] On the effects of intervention on money supplies in the ERM countries, see Mastropasqua, Micossi, and Rinaldi (1988).

[13] The Bundesbank stresses interest-rate policy more strongly than it did some years ago but continues to set monetary targets and pays close attention to them. Thus, the central bank that has the greatest freedom to pursue an independent monetary policy would seem to be using interest-rate policy to control the money supply (and to signal its determination to do so), whereas central banks that have less independence may really be using interest-rate policy to follow the Bundesbank and thus stabilize ERM exchange rates. They may be reluctant to say that, however, and thus make a virtue of necessity by describing interest-rate policy as a substitute for money-supply policy. (But this interpretation may be too simple, as the Bank of England shifted from monetary targeting to an interest-rate policy before sterling entered the ERM, forcing the Bank to pay close attention to German interest rates; the policy shift appears to have occurred before Nigel Lawson's attempt to "shadow the Deutschemark" in 1987-88.)

credit and one that seeks to influence the supply of credit?[14]

There can be no difference at all in a simple, partial-equilibrium model of the market for loanable funds. But that model omits two possibilities. On the one hand, a central bank that sets the interest rate and supplies reserves freely at that rate may forego the use of credit rationing by the banking system. If it aims instead at restricting reserves, it can intensify credit rationing and thus limit borrowing and spending by those whose demand for credit is interest-inelastic.[15] On the other hand, a policy that focuses on interest rates may have intramarginal effects on aggregate demand, by affecting old debtors as well as new borrowers, most notably those whose obligations have to be rolled over frequently or bear floating interest rates. These intramarginal effects may be stronger now than they used to be, because of the large debts borne by many firms and households.

One wonders, moreover, whether the current emphasis on interest-rate policy will last in Stage Three, after exchange rates have been locked. There will be no reason to worry about appropriate interest-rate differences across the ERM countries. The notion itself will cease to be meaningful. Furthermore, the ECB will have more control over the money supply of the ESCB countries as a group than individual central banks have currently over their own national money supplies. It will not have to peg the ECU by intervening on currency markets. Hence, attention may shift back to the quantity of credit and to monetary aggregates as proxies for it.

Methods of Monetary Management in the Major EC Countries
There are significant differences in the operating procedures of EC central banks. But many of these appear to reflect cross-country differences in the structures of national financial markets and in the asset holdings of credit institutions. Accordingly, the central banks' procedures have become more similar as those differences have diminished.[16] In fact, the four largest central banks—the Bundesbank, Banque de France, Banca d'Italia, and Bank of England—use the same basic methods in their day-to-day operations.

Each of the first three central banks has established a "corridor" for short-term interest rates. The corridor is bounded from below by the interest rate at which the central bank supplies liquidity on its own

---

[14] An analogous question was raised about monetary targeting. Was the aim to regulate the money supply, in and of itself, on the implicit supposition that the real-balance effect is large and reliable, or really to regulate the quantity of credit provided by the banking system? I take the second view in the next two paragraphs.

[15] This effect may not be very strong, however, unless large numbers of borrowers are bank-dependent. For a recent review of this and related issues, see Bernanke and Lown (1991) and the papers cited there, especially those by Bernanke and Blinder (1992) and Romer and Romer (1990).

[16] See Kneeshaw and Van de Bergh (1989) and Batten et al. (1990).

initiative by open-market operations (the repurchase rate on securities in the German case and the intervention rate in the French case); that rate is described here as the tender rate. The corridor is bounded from above by the interest rate at which the central bank supplies liquidity at the initiative of the banking system (the Lombard rate in the German case and the repurchase rate in the French case); that rate is often called the "penalty rate" but is described here as the lending rate. There are important differences, however, in the ways that these and other central banks conduct their open-market operations, and some use more than one technique.[17] Furthermore, EC central banks have different ways of lending to their banking systems; there are bank-by-bank limits in Italy and penalties for borrowing day after day, but no such limits or penalties in France or Germany. And some of the EC central banks, including the Bundesbank, have more than one credit facility.

The French, German, and Italian central banks deal directly with their banks, although other accredited financial institutions may participate in tenders held by the Banque de France. The Bank of England, by contrast, deals primarily with the London discount houses. Furthermore, the upper limit of the interest-rate corridor is not defined as sharply in the United Kingdom as it is in France, Germany, or Italy, because the Bank of England does not have a fixed lending rate. The interest rate at which it conducts its "2:30 lending" can change from day to day. But these differences are not fundamental. The liquidity provided by the Bank of England, through open-market operations and lending to the discount houses, flows on to the clearing banks as they call in their loans to the discount houses or sell bills to the discount houses.

As the ECB is supposed to use the national central banks to carry out its operations, it can be expected to adopt techniques similar to those used currently by the four largest central banks—all the more so, incidentally, because the smaller EC central banks have been adopting those techniques. Nevertheless, there will have to be some changes in the practices and balance sheets of the national central banks, and their size will depend on the *way* in which the ECB interprets the requirement that it use the national central banks. The ECB has also to decide whether to use reserve requirements.

Subsidiarity and Standardization

There are several ways of using the national central banks for open-market operations. Discussion has focused on three possibilities:

---

[17] In France and Germany, for example, open-market operations take place periodically; in Italy and the United Kingdom, the central banks operate more or less continuously. It would be hard for the ECB to keep close control over continuous operations conducted simultaneously by a number of national central banks. If it adopted the French or German method, however, the banking system might require large and liberal credit facilities to relieve cash shortages. Note in this connection that there are large differences in the degrees to which EC central banks

- A *centralized model* in which the terms and size of a tender would be decided by the ECB, bids would be collected by the national central banks from their domestic credit institutions, and the ECB would make the allotments.
- A *distributive model* in which the ECB would decide the size and terms but the global amount would be distributed among the national central banks, and they would conduct their own tenders.
- A *decentralized model* in which each national central bank would undertake its own open-market operations but would operate within two bands set by the ECB—one for its interest-rate instrument and one for its balance with the ECB.[18]

Note that all three models assume implicitly that each national central bank will continue to deal with its own domestic credit institutions—that French banks will not participate in tenders conducted by the Bundesbank, and so on.

Before looking at the problems raised by the first two models and, *a fortiori*, by an even more centralized model, consider the main problem raised by the third model. It appears to assume that there will continue to be some separation of national financial markets even in Stage Three. If there is instead a single, well-functioning ECB Funds market, arbitrage within that market will eradicate any incipient interest-rate difference produced by the central banks' open-market operations, and the decentralized model will serve mainly to produce large movements in the central banks' cash balances with the ECB. Hence, the national central banks would have to fine-tune their open-market operations to keep their cash balances within the bands set by the ECB.

Those balances will change, moreover, whenever there are net payments from one country to another. That was the lesson taught by Example A, above. Because the decentralized model would force the national central banks to offset those changes by varying the terms of their open-market operations, it could conceivably introduce unnecessary noise into the financial system and make it harder for market participants to read the signals sent by the ECB.

The same point can be made in terms used earlier. The decentralized model necessarily attaches normative importance to the central banks'

---

depend on open-market operations and direct lending to their banks. But these are hard to measure accurately because of different accounting practices. (When the Banque de France buys securities under a repurchase agreement, the securities remain with the bank selling them, and the books of the Banque de France show that it has made a loan to the seller, not an open-market purchase.) It should also be noted that different central banks buy different assets in their open-market operations. Most of them operate in government and commercial paper, but the Banco de España operates in its own CDs.

[18] Similar proposals were made by Thygesen (1989) and Ciampi (1989) but were intended for use in Stage Two, under the arrangements set forth in the Delors Report, which envisaged the creation of the ECB in Stage Two and its gradual involvement in monetary policy; see also Gros (1991).

balances with the ECB. But changes in those balances should be ignored in a monetary union. They are clearing balances, not reserve balances, and no one should pay any attention to them. If the operating rules of the ESCB say that the central banks' balances should not fluctuate widely (or should be balanced at the end of the day), fluctuations should be offset by transferring securities between the ECB and the national central banks, as they were at Step 4 in Example A. They should not be made by open-market operations, after the manner in which an independent central bank uses its monetary policy to defend its reserves.

If the decentralized model goes in the wrong direction, what must be done to go in the right direction? Should the ECB try to move directly to the centralized model? Or should it begin by moving to the distributive model and perhaps move later to the centralized model?

Evolutionary Standardization

In the early years of the Federal Reserve System, the individual Reserve Banks conducted their own open-market operations, mainly to acquire income-producing assets. It took many years to coordinate those operations fully, and many more years to make them the main instrument of monetary policy.[19] The ECB will not have this problem. Its Statute gives it full control of monetary policy and of the instruments required to conduct it. The governors of the national central banks, however, will have more influence in the ECB than the presidents of the Federal Reserve Banks in the United States; they will all be voting members of the Governing Council, where they will outnumber the members of the Executive Board. And they would surely oppose any arrangement that gave some of the national central banks more prominence than others or favored the use of some countries' markets.[20] Hence, the ECB is less likely to adopt a centralized model than a distributive model and quite unlikely to adopt an arrangement of the sort used in the United States, where the Federal Reserve Bank of New York acts on behalf of the whole Federal Reserve System.

Furthermore, the distributive model may better suited to the conditions prevailing early in Stage Three. It cannot give way to a centralized model until certain conditions are fulfilled.

Two conditions were introduced at the beginning of this chapter. There must be an ECB Funds market, where credit institutions can lend and borrow ECU-denominated balances held at the national central banks, and there must be well-integrated markets in ECU-denominated bills and

---

[19] See Eichengreen (1991a). Even after they were coordinated fully, open-market operations did not displace discount-window lending as the main instrument of monetary management. In fact, that did not really happen until the 1951 Accord, which freed the Federal Reserve from its obligation to support the prices of US Government securities.

[20] Recall the point made in Chapter II, however, that the ESCB Statute does not indicate clearly whether decisions of this sort will be made by the Council or the Board.

bonds. But a third condition must also be met. Credit institutions must have in their portfolios adequate supplies of the securities traded most extensively on the integrated markets. If these three conditions are not met, the effects of open-market operations will not spread speedily or evenly across the ESCB countries.

The roles of the first two conditions were illustrated by the examples presented earlier; they are needed to disseminate the liquidity provided by open-market operations. It may be possible, moreover, to fulfil them quickly in Stage Three by following the two suggestions made at the start of this chapter—that the ECB and national central banks should denominate their balance sheets in ECU and that ECU endorsements should be attached to all government securities and other debt instruments bought by the ESCB. It may be harder, however, to fulfil the third condition quickly. Some countries' banks will not hold the securities most likely to be traded on integrated markets and used in open-market operations by the major central banks. Hence, the ECB may have to distribute its open-market operations among the national central banks at the beginning of Stage Three, and they may have to go on using somewhat different methods in order to accommodate the cross-country differences in the portfolios of credit institutions. Those differences will diminish during Stage Two but not by enough to be ignored completely at the outset of Stage Three.

From the very start, however, the ECB could tilt the distribution of its open-market operation in favor of centralization. By giving disproportionately large allocations to the central banks in the main financial centers, it can encourage other countries' credit institutions to use those major centers and adapt their own portfolios accordingly. To this end, however, it must insist from the outset that all credit institutions should be free to participate on equal terms in the tenders conducted by the national central banks.[21] The ECB might also want to encourage EC governments to standardize the terms of the securities they issue—a process that could benefit the governments too, by giving them access to the most efficient markets.

To carry standardization further, the ECB could foster competition among the national central banks. If banks could participate on equal terms in tenders conducted outside their own countries—if French banks could sell bills directly to the Bundesbank—the banks would take their business to the most efficient centers, and that would have two consequences. First, the banks would have more incentive to adapt their own portfolios— to build up their holdings of the debt instruments used in the most efficient centers. Second, they would make less use of the more expensive tenders.

---

21 This rule would also give effect to the requirement in Article 2 of the ESCB Statute that it "act in accordance with the principle of an open market economy with free competition" and would attack the restrictive practices of some countries' banks. (Each national central bank would have to retain the right to judge the creditworthiness of the institutions seeking to do business with it, but it could not discriminate by nationality.)

Business would come to be concentrated at the national central banks having the most attractive methods, and the ECB, in turn, could shift the distribution of its open-market operations in favor of those central banks. It could do that by raising the shares of those central banks whose tenders were, on average, most heavily oversubscribed.[22]

Some central banks that lost out in this competition might not be able to do much about it. Others might alter their methods. If intermediation by the discount market made it more expensive for banks to sell bills in London, the Bank of England would lose business to other central banks, and it might decide to open its tenders directly to banks, rather than conduct them through the discount houses. The discount houses would have to adapt—find new work to do—but adaptation forced by competition would be easier to justify than adaptation forced by fiat of the ECB.

Would this evolutionary process necessarily culminate in the complete centralization of ECB operations? Not necessarily. Every national central bank might still perform two vital tasks.

First, each central bank might continue to engage in direct, short-term lending to credit institutions. That is the practice in the United States, where each Federal Reserve Bank makes loans at its discount window to those banks that hold reserves at that Reserve Bank. But the central banks would have to charge identical lending rates and impose similar restrictions, if any, on the amounts of credit made available this way. Otherwise, there would be profit opportunities for credit institutions with access to the central bank that lent at the lowest rate. There might appear to be potential conflict between the decentralization of direct lending and ECB control over monetary policy. It should be remembered, however, that the central banks' lending rate would continue to be the upper bound of an interest-rate corridor and that the volume of lending at that rate would be determined by the ECB's own policies. Large numbers of credit institutions would borrow from their central banks if, and only if, the ECB raised the ECB Funds rate by cutting back its open-market purchases or making open-market sales.

Second, each central bank might initiate open-market operations to offset the effects of its government's financial operations on the liquidity of the institutions that keep their cash balances with that central bank. The

---

[22] The ECB would have to choose a rule to govern the initial distribution of its open-market operations. The rule might be based on the key defined in Article 29 of the ESCB Statute for distributing the capital of the ECB. Alternatively, it might be based on the shares of the national central banks in their total "monetary" assets (i.e., those used in Article 32 of the ESCB Statute to define the "monetary income" of the national central banks); those shares are distorted now by cross-country differences in reserve requirements, but the differences would be eliminated in Stage Three, when reserve requirements would be standardized if they were used at all. Note that the arrangements discussed here assume implicitly that the ECB will focus on the supply of reserves to the banking system and imply that the national central banks will use volume tenders rather than price tenders in their open market operations.

principal effects of the government's cash flows will still be localized,[23] and the national central bank is likely to have the most timely information on their size and sign. But operations of this sort would have to aim at offsetting those cash flows completely, even if they cannot do so perfectly in practice. If given discretion to offset *some* of the cash flows, national central banks might act in ways that produce uncertainty about the stance of monetary policy.

Why Asset Composition Should Not Matter

Under Article 104 of the Treaty, the ECB is barred from lending directly to governments or buying securities directly from them. Critics of this rule have argued that it is too narrow. If it is designed to protect the ECB from having to engage in "monetary financing" of budget deficits, the ECB should also be barred from buying government securities in the secondary market.[24] It should limit its open-market operations to commercial paper and similar instruments.

The validity of this objection, however, depends on the true purpose of the prohibition, and two interpretations are possible. It may be meant to reinforce the ban on "excessive" budget deficits contained in Article 104c of the Treaty and discussed in the next chapter. Alternatively, it may be meant to reinforce the ability of the ECB to control the money supply.

On the first interpretation, Article 104 may be too narrow in one sense, because it does not cover open-market purchases, but too broad in another sense. It should apply exclusively to governments that violate the prohibition on excessive deficits. In other words, it should find its way onto the list of sanctions that the EC can apply when a government fails to correct an excessive deficit.[25] Because the ban on monetary financing is not selective and appears in the Treaty before the prohibition on excessive deficits, this first interpretation does not stand up well.

On the second interpretation, that the ban on monetary financing is meant chiefly to protect the integrity of monetary policy, Article 104 is not too narrow and should not be extended to open-market purchases. An open-ended obligation to make loans to governments or to purchase securities directly from them would prevent the ECB from controlling the money supply effectively. But the right of the ECB to buy government securities in the secondary market, exercised at its discretion, cannot have that effect. Indeed, a ban on open-market purchases would unduly restrict

---

[23] That is not the case, of course, in the United States, where there is only one national government, whose cash flows are much larger and fluctuate more sharply than those of the state governments.

[24] See Neumann (1991).

[25] The list includes a recommendation to the European Investment Bank (EIB) that the recalcitrant country be barred from further EIB borrowing. It could have included a recommendation to the ECB that it make no additional open-market purchases of the recalcitrant country's securities. Admittedly, any such recommendation, even if nonbinding, might be seen to infringe on the independence of the ECB.

the independence of the ECB.[26] On this interpretation, in fact, the ban on direct purchases may be too broad; it could be confined to obligatory purchases.

These considerations lead one to conclude that the ECB need not pay much attention to the asset composition of its open-market purchases, and three more considerations support this conclusion.

First, the rules for distributing the interest income of the ESCB will not favor a country whose securities bulk large in the total portfolio of the ESCB. The larger the holdings of Italian debt, for example, the larger the interest payments that Italy must make to the ESCB. But the share of the Banca d'Italia in the total income of the ESCB will be proportional to its share in the total capital of the ECB.[27] Hence, open-market purchases of Italian debt will generate interest-income transfers from Italy to other ESCB countries, and there will no reason to accuse the ESCB of favoring Italy when it buys Italian debt.

Second, the distribution of open-market operations is not apt to affect the structure of interest rates substantially. Once government securities have been redenominated in ECU, interest rates on individual issues will differ only insofar as the issues themselves differ in default risk, taxability, and liquidity. They will not be very responsive to transitory changes in demand or supply. The ESCB could perhaps affect the structure of interest rates if it did most of its business in one country's bills or bonds and was expected to do so regularly; it would deepen the market for them, impart more liquidity to them, and might thus reduce their interest rates relative to others. But it would have to concentrate heavily and regularly on those securities to make much difference on this score. (The effect would be small in any case if the ESCB conducted most of its open-market operations in short-term securities, where liquidity premia are not likely to be large.)

Finally, it must be remembered that the open-market purchases of the ESCB will be fairly small compared to total stocks of debt outstanding. If the domestic assets of the ESCB were made to grow at 5 percent per year and *all* of the growth resulted from open-market purchases of Italian government debt—the unrealistic but limiting case—the ESCB's net acquisitions would be no larger than 2 percent per year of the outstanding stock of debt.[28]

---

[26] It should be noted, moreover, that Article 104b of the Treaty, which says that the EC will not "bail out" governments or other public entities by assuring liability for their obligations, does not prevent the ECB from purchasing those obligations in the open market, and it may want to do that in order to serve as lender of last resort in the broad sense suggested by Chapter II.

[27] The allocation of the "monetary income" of the national central banks is governed by Article 32 of the ESCB Statute; the allocation of net profit or loss of the ECB is governed by Article 33. But the same basic rule is used to distribute the two types of income.

[28] At the end of 1989, the domestic claims of all EC central banks—direct lending plus holdings of securities—amounted to about 336 billion ECU, and the Italian government debt amounted to about 786 billion ECU.

At the start of Stage Three, of course, the asset composition of open-market purchases will be determined largely by their distribution among the national central banks, because of the basic reason for distributing those purchases—the differences in assets held by banks in different countries. Thereafter, however, the ECB may want to adopt broad guidelines to achieve some sort of balance in the composition of total ESCB assets, so as to avoid any appearance of arbitrary or biased behavior. But that would be the only reason for giving the matter any attention.

The Use and Application of Reserve Requirements

Although central banks in Europe use similar techniques to manage money-market conditions and thus influence interest rates, they differ in another way. Reserve requirements are used in France, Germany, Italy, and most other EC countries, but not in the United Kingdom.

Those who were taught that the money supply depends on the stock of bank reserves and the deposit multiplier, which depends on the reserve requirement, find it hard to believe that the money supply can behave in a non-explosive way unless it is constrained by reserve requirements. But it does not behave much differently in Britain than in other countries.

The existence and stability of a finite deposit multiplier does not depend on the use of reserve requirements. It is sufficient to have a stable relationship between the demand for currency and the total money stock, so that part of any increase in the banks' cash balances at the central bank will leak into currency holdings by the public. In an open economy with a pegged exchange rate, moreover, large external leakages will curb the growth of the money supply; an increase in the banks' cash balances will be eroded gradually by capital outflows, which must lead to official intervention on the foreign-exchange market. (Alternatively, the anticipation of capital outflows and reserve losses will deter the central bank from increasing the banks' cash balances; the multiplier may be high, but it will have nothing to multiply.)

It can even be argued that the rule used by the Bank of England gives it more control over money-market conditions than the rules used by most other countries. British banks must balance their cash positions on a daily basis; they cannot run overdrafts from one day to the next. In most countries with reserve requirements, by contrast, banks must meet them on average in each accounting period but can have deficiencies within the period.

Some central banks acknowledge that reserve requirements are not truly necessary for short-term monetary management—not even for long-term control over the supply of money. They recognize, indeed, that reserve requirements may reduce their control of the money supply by driving domestic deposits offshore, where they are not subject to reserve requirements. Nevertheless, they appear to believe that reserve requirements give them more leverage and allow them to control monetary conditions without having to intervene as heavily or frequently as might be required under alternative arrangements. When banks are allowed to have short-term reserve deficiencies, the central bank is relieved of the need to intervene on a daily basis; it can supply or withdraw reserves periodically and allow the banks to adjust thereafter.[29] Accordingly, national central banks that use reserve requirements are likely to press for their adoption by the ECB rather than agree to abandon them.

If the ECB uses reserve requirements, it will have to impose them uniformly. It will also have to decide whether to impose them on a host-country (decentralized) basis or a home-country (consolidated) basis.

At present, European central banks typically impose their reserve requirements on home-currency deposits at domestic branches of domestic and foreign banks. They exempt home-currency deposits at the foreign branches of domestic banks, as well as all foreign-currency deposits. This treatment is consistent with the principle embodied in the Basle Concordat and the Second Banking Directive—that rules relating to liquidity should be administered on a host-country (decentralized) basis, whereas rules relating to solvency should be administered on a home-country (consolidated) basis.

With the advent of a single currency, however, there may be reason to reconsider. The distinction between home and foreign currencies will be obliterated in respect of EC currencies, so that most of the present foreign-currency deposits will be subject automatically to reserve requirements, and the requirements will be uniform. But the jurisdictional question will crop up differently. German banks will have to hold reserves against the ECU deposit liabilities of their French branches, but should they hold them with the Banque de France or the Bundesbank?

If all of the major EC countries participate in the monetary union, it will not make much difference, and administrative convenience might then dictate a shift to home-country (consolidated) reserve accounting. That is the practice in the United States; a bank with branches in two or more Federal Reserve Districts holds its required reserves with the Reserve Bank for the district in which it has its head office.[30] But matters are more complicated if some EC countries do not participate.

Suppose that the United Kingdom does not participate and that reserves do not earn interest.

Under host-country reserve accounting, the banks of ESCB countries would have an incentive to book ECU deposits in London, as they would

---

[29] Recall the point made in an earlier footnote that this is the practice in France and Germany.

[30] A separately incorporated subsidiary, however, holds its reserves with the Reserve Bank for the district in which it has its own head office.

not have to hold reserves against them and thus would not be handicapped vis-à-vis British banks in competing for that business. But UK banks would have no incentive to attract ECU deposits by opening branches in ESCB countries, as those deposits would be subject to reserve requirements. The ECB's control over the volume of ECU deposits would thus be limited by the existence of a large off-shore market in London—which would be a significant limitation. But there would be no limitation on its control over the volume of ECU deposits held at banks in the ESCB countries.

Under home-country reserve accounting, by contrast, the banks of ESCB countries would have no incentive to book ECU deposits in London, and the off-shore market would be dominated by British and foreign banks, but that market would probably be smaller. But UK banks would have an incentive to compete for ECU deposits in the ESCB countries, as they would not have to hold reserves against them. In fact, they would want to take full advantage of their rights under the Second Banking Directive. This might limit sharply the ECB's control over the volume of ECU deposits in the ESCB countries, and that limitation might be more serious than the one produced by a larger off-shore market.

If reserves earned interest at a market rate, the whole problem would vanish. But the central banks most likely to insist that the ECB use reserve requirements are the ones most likely to resist that innovation.[31] It may thus be imprudent for the ESCB to switch from host-country to home-country accounting, even though the latter would be less cumbersome.

---

[31] Recall that Community legislation will be required to set the deposit base and maximum reserve ratio, but no provision is made in the Treaty for legislation to set a minimum interest rate. That was suggested but rejected.

Appendix—Additional Banking Transactions

This appendix uses the framework set out in the text to illustrate additional transactions. Four transactions are considered here:

I. Intervention in the foreign-exchange market via the Banque de France.

II. Intervention in the foreign-exchange market directly by the ECB.

III. A switch by Jean from franc to mark deposits.

IV. A switch by Jean from French to German securities.

As in the text, entries are changes in balance-sheet items expressed in ECU equivalents.

Intervention in the Foreign-Exchange Market via the Banque de France
Suppose that the ECB decides to buy dollars in the foreign-exchange market in order to prevent appreciation of the ECU (and of the participants' national currencies) and that the Banque de France is instructed to buy the dollars for its own account. As with an open-market purchase, the immediate results depend on the identity of the counterparty selling the dollars. If the counterparty is a foreign-exchange dealer wanting to buy francs and holding an account with the Banque Nationale de Paris, the results will be those shown in Example I, and they resemble those shown at Step 1 of Example B in the text (except that the Banque Nationale de Paris' balance

---

**Appendix Example I:
Purchase of Dollars by the European Central Bank via the Banque de France**

Banque de France

Assets		Liabilities	
➡ Dollar Reserves	+100	ECU Deposit owed to Banque Nationale de Paris	+100

Banque Nationale de Paris

Assets		Liabilities	
ECU Deposit with Banque de France	+100	FF Deposit owed to Foreign Exchange Dealer	+100

All Amounts Are Changes in ECU Equivalents

---

sheet shows an increase in deposit liabilities to the foreign-exchange dealer rather than a fall in securities held by the Banque Nationale de Paris).

If the counterparty wants to buy marks, the results will resemble those shown in Example C of the text. (Alternatively, the ECB might instruct the Bundesbank to execute the transaction in place of the Banque de France.)

Intervention in the Foreign-Exchange Market Directly by the ECB
If the ECB decides to buy dollars for its own account, the results will be those shown in Example II, and they resemble those shown in Example D of the text, where the ECB made an open-market purchase for its own account.

A Switch from Franc to Mark Deposits
When exchange rates are fixed irrevocably, there is no reason for anyone to shift from one currency to another, apart from reasons of convenience. If there are doubts about the irrevocability of the fixing, however, there can be a "run" from one currency into another.

Suppose that Jean distrusts the irrevocability of the fixing and thus switches from franc deposits at the Banque Nationale de Paris to mark deposits at the Commerzbank. The immediate effects are shown in Example III, together with the transfers of securities needed to balance the positions of the Banque de France and Bundesbank vis-à-vis the ECB. They resemble

---

Appendix Example II:
Purchase of Dollars by the European Central Bank for Its Own Account

European Central Bank

Assets		Liabilities	
Dollar Reserves	+100	ECU Deposit owed to Banque de France	+100

Banque de France

Assets		Liabilities	
ECU Deposit at European Central Bank	+100	ECU Deposit owed to Banque Nationale de Paris	+100

Banque Nationale de Paris

Assets		Liabilities	
ECU Deposit at Banque de France	+100	FF Deposit owed to Foreign-Exchange Dealer	+100

All Amounts Are Changes in ECU Equivalents

59

closely the effects of a payment from Jean to Karl combined with a corresponding transfers of securities, shown at Step 4 of Example A in the text. (The only difference is the ownership of the deposit appearing on the liability side of the Commerzbank balance sheet, which belongs to Jean, not Karl.)

There is no change in the total money supply of the ESCB countries, only in its currency composition, and no need for the central banks to take other steps. They have merely to treat the transfers of securities to and from the ECB as being routine matters, quite different from liquidity or balance-of-payments support.

How far can this process go? Under an ordinary fixed-rate system, no central bank can defend its currency indefinitely. It will exhaust its

---

Appendix Example III:
Currency Substitution by Jean

European Central Bank

Assets	Liabilities
DM Securities (ECU endorsed) -100	ECU Deposit owed to Banque de France -100
FF Securities (ECU endorsed) +100	ECU Deposit owed to Bundesbank +100

Banque de France

Assets	Liabilities
ECU Deposit at European Central Bank -100	ECU Deposit owed to Banque Nationale de Paris -100
FF Securities (ECU endorsed) -100	

Bundesbank

Assets	Liabilities
ECU Deposit at European Central Bank +100	ECU Deposit owed to Commerzbank +100
DM Securities (ECU endorsed) +100	

Banque Nationale de Paris

Assets	Liabilities
➡ ECU Deposit at Banque de France -100	FF Deposit owed to Jean -100

Commerzbank

Assets	Liabilities
ECU Deposit at Bundesbank +100	DM Deposit owed to Jean +100

All Amounts Are Changes in ECU Equivalents
Shaded Entries Are Changes Reversed
During the Sequence of Transactions

---

foreign-exchange reserves before the "Jeans" have withdrawn all of their deposits. There are no such reserves in the examples studied here. But an analogous problem may arise eventually. The Banque Nationale de Paris may exhaust its balance at the Banque de France and its ability to borrow in the ECB Funds market. At that point, the Banque de France must start to buy securities from the Banque Nationale de Paris (or make loans to it) and must transfer securities to the ECB to balance its own account at the ECB. This process can continue for as long as the Banque Nationale de Paris has assets it can sell (or pledge) to the Banque de France. If the Banque Nationale de Paris is solvent, of course, its assets will exceed its deposit liabilities. Its problem is to mobilize those assets, and the solution to that problem rests with the Banque de France, which must buy them (or accept them as collateral) to defend the irrevocably fixed exchange rate

---

Appendix Example IV:
Asset Substitution by Jean

European Central Bank

Assets		Liabilities	
DM Securities (ECU endorsed)	-100	ECU Deposit owed to	
FF Securities (ECU endorsed)	+100	Banque de France	-100
		ECU Deposit owed to Bundesbank	+100

Banque de France

Assets		Liabilities	
ECU Deposit at European Central Bank	-100	ECU Deposit owed to Banque Nationale de Paris	-100
FF Securities (ECU endorsed)	-100		

Bundesbank

Assets		Liabilities	
ECU Deposit at ECB	+100	ECU Deposit owed to Commerzbank	+100
DM Securities (ECU endorsed)	+100		

Banque Nationale de Paris

Assets		Liabilities	
➡ ECU Deposit at Banque de France	-100	FF Deposit owed to Jean	+100
		FF Deposit owed to Anne	-100

Commerzbank

Assets		Liabilities	
ECU Deposit at Bundesbank	+100	DM Deposit owed to Karl	+100

All Amounts Are Changes in ECU Equivalents
Shaded Entries Are Changes Reversed
During the Sequence of Transactions

against speculative pressure.

But doubts about the irrevocability of the fixed exchange rates could cause Jean to sell off other franc-denominated assets (presumably those that do not have an ECU endorsement—although he might have doubts about those too). This possibility is examined in the next example.

A Switch from Franc to Mark Bonds

To switch from franc to mark bonds, Jean must sell his franc bonds for francs, buy marks, and then sell the marks for mark bonds. Assume for simplicity that he sells the franc bonds to Anne, another French resident, and buys the mark bonds from Karl. The results are shown in Example IV, together with the transfers of securities within the ESCB. They differ from those in Example III in only two small ways. (1) The reduction in franc deposits shown on the books of the Banque Nationale de Paris is the reduction in Anne's deposit resulting from her purchase of bonds from Jean. (2) The increase in mark deposits shown on the books of the Commerzbank is the increase in Karl's deposit resulting from his sale of bonds to Jean.

If Anne becomes increasingly reluctant to buy franc bonds from Jean, the interest rate on those bonds will rise, curbing Jean's appetite for mark bonds. Even if that does not happen, however, and the process of asset substitution continues, it need not jeopardize the fixed-rate system, so long as the Banque de France is willing to replenish the cash reserves of the Banque Nationale de Paris.

IV. Fiscal Policy and EMU

In the 1970s, research and debate on macroeconomic issues focused mainly on monetary policy. In the 1980s, they shifted to fiscal policy, and much of the debate about EMU has focused on the implications of monetary union for the conduct, financing, and coordination of national fiscal policies.

The Dimensions of Fiscal Policy

An analysis of fiscal policy must have three macroeconomic dimensions. It must cover the stabilization problem, the policy-mix problem, and the solvency problem. All three take on special forms in a monetary union.[1]

The Stabilization Problem

When a country joins a monetary union, forgoing the use of monetary and exchange-rate policies to stabilize its national economy, the independent use of fiscal policy becomes more attractive, despite the political obstacles to fiscal flexibility. It is indeed the only policy instrument available for dealing with country-specific shocks—disturbances different in nature or timing from those affecting other members of the union—and with common shocks that have asymmetric effects on individual members of the union.

It is easy to devise hypothetical cases in which fiscal policies, used independently, can offset those shocks without harming other members of the monetary union or leading them to alter their own fiscal policies. It is

---

[1] Surveys of the literature on these problems as they relate to EMU are provided by the Commission (1990) and van der Ploeg (1991a). A fourth fiscal problem lies on the boundary between the macro and micro dimensions—how EMU will affect the size of the public sector and the supply of public goods. Some believe that it may shrink the public sector. Thus, van

also easy, however, to devise cases in which a fiscal-policy change has adverse effects on other members of the union or provokes them to make policy changes of their own that nullify the effects of the initial policy change. The likelihood of this second outcome is increased by "model uncertainty" and the vagaries of the political process, which make it hard for governments to change their fiscal policies by the right amounts and at the right times.[2]

Much recent research on the stabilization problem in EMU has taken as its point of departure the notion of an "optimum currency area" as defined by Mundell (1961). Two countries may be said to constitute an optimum currency area when the fixing of the nominal exchange rate between their currencies does not impose real costs on their economies. That will be the case, of course, if both countries' prices are perfectly flexible; the *real* exchange rate will be flexible even though the nominal exchange rate is fixed. It will also be the case, however, if labor and capital are perfectly mobile between them. A switch in demand between the two countries' exports will reduce the demand for labor and capital in one country and raise it in the other, but that will not pose problems if labor and capital move promptly from the first country to the second. Put differently, a currency area is optimal if participation does not raise the members' need to use their fiscal policies for domestic stabilization—if it does not raise their vulnerability to real shocks or diminish their ability to deal with them.

Clearly, there can be no optimum currency area in the strictest sense. Prices are not perfectly flexible, and labor and capital are not perfectly mobile. And Europe is far from being an optimum currency area in this strict sense, because labor mobility is fairly low. It may rise in the years ahead, after the completion of the internal market, but will still be limited by linguistic and cultural barriers.[3] This conclusion, however, does not tell

---

der Ploeg (1991b) argues that monetary union will reduce revenues from seigniorage, while the completion of the internal market will reduce tax revenues by raising factor mobility and fostering tax competition. On tax competition, see Giovannini (1989) and Eichengreen (1990b); on seigniorage, see Drazen (1989) and Grilli (1989). (Note that both phenomena could cause more borrowing, not less spending, and are thus cited by those who fear unsustainable growth in stocks of government debt.) Casella (1990) provides a model in which governments acting independently produce excessive quantities of public goods, so that fiscal-policy coordination is needed for an optimal outcome. In her model, moreover, a monetary union can substitute for fiscal coordination. I have shown, however, that Casella's findings flow from her assumption that governments are indifferent between creating money and using taxes to finance the production of public goods; see Kenen (1991b). When money creation and taxation are not perfect substitutes, a monetary union cannot substitute for explicit fiscal-policy coordination. In fact, a monetary union by itself leads them to produce too few public goods.

[2] The notion of "model uncertainty" encompasses all of the gaps in our understanding of economic behavior and the international transmission process. Its implications for policy coordination have been discussed extensively (see, e.g., Frankel, 1988, and Bryant et al., 1988), but it is no less relevant to the conduct of national fiscal policy in an open-economy setting.

[3] Eichengreen (1990a) surveys the evidence suggesting that labor mobility is lower between EC countries than between regions in the United States or Canada. In Eichengreen (1992b), he

us very much. It takes no account of the benefits from monetary union and ignores some other considerations that bear on the costs of participation and on the need for using fiscal policy to maintain domestic economic stability.

If national economies are highly diversified, industry-specific shocks need not add up into country-specific shocks. They may tend to average out. If the economies are similar, moreover, they will experience similar shocks and can alter their common monetary policy or their common exchange rate to offset those shocks. Hence, the higher the degrees of diversification and economic similarity, the lower the costs of monetary union.[4]

More generally, the real economic costs of monetary union will depend on the size and nature of the shocks impinging on the national economies, given the amounts of price flexibility and factor mobility. If they are small and symmetric, the costs will be low; if they are large and asymmetric, the costs will be high. This proposition has led to much empirical work on the nature and size of the shocks experienced by EC countries, compared to those experienced by individual regions in the United States and in other multi-regional countries, which can be viewed for this purpose as monetary unions.[5]

Bayoumi and Eichengreen (1992) segregate demand and supply shocks by using assumptions about the paths followed by prices and output in response to those shocks. (Demand shocks are deemed to have transitory effects on output and permanent effects on prices; supply shocks are deemed to have permanent effects on both.) Applying this approach to individual EC countries and US regions, Bayoumi and

---

offers new evidence that internal mobility is much higher in the United States than in Great Britain or Italy.

[4] The first possibility was raised in Kenen (1969), and both possibilities are cited by the Commission (1990) as reasons for believing that the costs of EMU will not be very high. But recent work on geography and trade suggests that further integration in Europe may lead to greater specialization rather than greater diversification; see Krugman (1991) and Bayoumi and Eichengreen (1992). Furthermore, Masson and Melitz (1990) remind us that countries facing common shocks may want to respond to them differently if they have different policy preferences.

[5] Eichengreen (1990a) inspired much of this work with his comprehensive survey of US experience; other important contributions include Lamfalussy (1989), De Grauwe and Vanhaverbeke (1991), Eichengreen (1991b), Weber (1991), and Bayoumi and Eichengreen (1992). As Eichengreen (1991b) points out, however, some of these studies are flawed, because they use changes in real exchange rates to measure asymmetric shocks. Changes in real exchange rates are endogenous responses to shocks, and their sizes will therefore depend on the availability of other ways to adjust to shocks, not merely the sizes of the shocks themselves. If two countries or regions make up an optimum currency area in the strict Mundellian sense, the real exchange rate between their currencies will be stable in the face of large asymmetric shocks. As the studies by Bayoumi and Eichengreen (1992) and Weber (1991) come closest to avoiding this methodological problem, they are the ones featured in the text. (Weber's study, however, treats every change in every variable—including a number of endogenous variables—as a separate shock, whereas Bayoumi and Eichengreen treat each such change as reflecting current and past shocks.)

Eichengreen conclude that demand shocks affecting EC countries are smaller than those affecting US regions, whereas supply shocks affecting the EC "core" are similar in size to those affecting US regions, but those affecting the EC "periphery" are uniformly larger. (The "core" comprises the original ERM members except Italy, which had a wide exchange-rate band during the period under study.) They also find, however, that the correlation of demand shocks across EC countries is lower than across US regions, and this is likewise true for supply shocks. In other words, EC shocks are less symmetric than US shocks. But the supply-shock correlations are higher for the EC core, which says that the shocks are more symmetric, leading Bayoumi and Eichengreen to suggest that there is a case for a two-speed approach to monetary union, with the core countries moving faster.

Weber (1991) uses a different way to measure and appraise the shocks affecting EC countries.[6] He finds that shocks to inflation rates and other nominal variables are highly symmetric and that the asymmetric components have been shrinking, and he notes that this process should continue under EMU. Supply shocks have likewise been fairly symmetric. But demand shocks and labor-market shocks have been sufficiently asymmetric to justify using fiscal policies for domestic stabilization.

State governments in the United States, however, do not use fiscal policy for that purpose. Most of them operate under self-imposed rules that make them balance their annual budgets. These range from strong restrictions on actual borrowing to weak rules requiring the state's governor to submit a balanced budget; see von Hagen (1991). Hence, the states' fiscal systems tend to operate procyclically, not contracyclically; a state must cut spending or raise tax rates whenever a recession reduces its tax revenues. The federal fiscal system, however, compensates in part for this perversity of the states' fiscal systems. Whenever economic activity falls in an individual state or region, its citizens' federal tax payments fall and they receive more federal transfer payments.[7]

This phenomenon was identified by Ingram (1959, 1973) and has been studied closely by those seeking to contrast fiscal arrangements in federal systems with those in the EC. The first such study, by Sala-i-Martin and Sachs (1991), found that a region's tax payments to the US federal government fall by about 34 cents when its per capita income falls by one dollar, while transfers to the region rise by about 6 cents. The two figures

---

6 The methodology is adapted from Cohen and Wyplosz (1989).

7 Note that this flexibility has two parts—an effect on the distribution of federal receipts and payments and an effect on their levels. Suppose that the federal budget is balanced initially. If economic activity falls in one region but rises in another, the redistribution of federal receipts and payments can help to stabilize activity in both regions without causing the federal government to run a surplus or deficit. If activity falls in one region without rising in another, the changes in federal receipts and payments can still help that region but will cause the federal government to run a deficit. In effect, the federal government will borrow on behalf of the region suffering the fall in activity (and it can typically borrow on less costly terms than those the regional authorities would face).

together say that the net change in federal receipts and payments offsets about 40 cents of a one-dollar fall in regional income. But von Hagen (1991) criticized that study for failing to distinguish between structural and cyclical effects; high-income regions can be expected to pay more taxes than low-income regions, and this structural effect may have contaminated the attempt by Sachs and Sala-i-Martin to measure the cyclical effect. And von Hagen's own figures for the cyclical effect are much lower. But Bayoumi and Masson (1991) also try to distinguish between structural and cyclical effects and come up with different numbers; cyclical changes in federal receipts and payments offset about 28 cents of a one-dollar fall in income—a figure lower than the number produced by Sala-i-Martin and Sachs but higher than the number produced by von Hagen. Turning to Canadian experience, however, Bayoumi and Masson find a smaller fiscal effect (about 17 cents on the dollar).

Changes in federal receipts and payments cannot offset asymmetric shocks completely, but their contribution is not negligible. Recall the point made by the Delors Report (1989), however, concerning the European situation. As the EC budget is small and does not have much cyclical flexibility, the stabilization problem will have to be faced at the national level—albeit with strong safeguards at the EC level to protect the fiscal stance of the EC as a whole.[8]

The Policy-Mix Problem

The small size of the EC budget means that the sum of the national surpluses and deficits will determine the fiscal stance of the Community. When combined with the monetary policy of the ECB, it will therefore define the policy mix. The policy mix, in turn, will influence the national economies of the member countries, whatever they may do about their own fiscal policies, and it also will influence the world economy, because it will affect ECU exchange rates and world interest rates.

Recall the example in Chapter III, where a large EC country ran a big budget deficit. If the ECB does not alter its monetary policy when that deficit emerges, EC interest rates will rise, crowding out domestic investment in every EC country, and a capital inflow will cause the ECU to appreciate, crowding out the production of tradable goods by reducing exports and raising imports.

---

[8] It is sometimes suggested that the Community's structural funds could be used to cushion the effects of asymmetric disturbances. These proposals, however, confuse stabilization with convergence and cohesion. The structural funds are meant to reduce basic disparities in levels of economic development, not to offset short-term fluctuations in activity and income. Eichengreen (1991b), Masson and Melitz (1990), and Wypiosz (1991) would make the EC budget more flexible by shifting some social insurance programs, notably unemployment insurance, from the national to the EC level. Masson and Melitz rightly point out that the US fiscal system was not designed for regional stabilization; its contribution is a by-product of ways in which it treats individual citizens. Therefore, it does not generate inter-regional conflict. By implication, the centralization of social insurance programs would be less controversial than use of the structural funds for contracyclical stabilization.

These effects may not be large enough to reduce output and employment in the country running the deficit; the outcome will depend on the size of the increase in domestic demand resulting from the deficit, compared to the crowding-out effects on investment and trade flows. They are more likely to reduce output and employment in other EC countries, which may not experience a comparable increase in demand on account of the budget deficit but are sure to share the crowding-out effects. The net effect on the outside world is hardest to predict, because the increase in world interest rates will reduce investment but the appreciation of the ECU will stimulate production in the tradable-goods sector. Uncertainty about the signs of these effects, however, does not diminish the significance of the change in the policy mix for capital formation and the composition of aggregate demand in the EC as a whole.

The recommendations in the Delors Report (1989) were aimed partly at this problem and its implications for the economic environment in which the ECB will function. It called for fiscal-policy coordination as well as binding limits on individual budget deficits. Without them, it said, the EC cannot expect to establish a policy mix appropriate for internal balance and cannot play its part in the global adjustment process.

The Solvency Problem

A debtor can be said to be solvent if the debtor's obligations are not larger than the present value of the revenue stream available to service them. The main difference between public and private debtors derives from the difference in their revenue streams. Governments can increase taxes. Other debtors cannot.

The basic solvency constraint can be reformulated in terms which say that the growth rate of debt must not exceed the interest rate on the debt. In the case of a government, the growth rate of debt is defined for this purpose as the ratio of the budget deficit (excluding interest payments) to the stock of debt outstanding. This reformulation can then be used to ask whether a government's fiscal stance is sustainable. Calculations of this sort, with several refinements, have been made by Corsetti and Roubini (1991), who find that solvency is not a problem for most of the large EC countries. But it is a problem for Italy and for several smaller countries, including Greece, Belgium, Ireland, and the Netherlands.[9]

If markets were able to price risk accurately, governments would find it increasingly expensive to borrow as their deficits and debts drove them toward the boundary of the solvency constraint, and there is some evidence to this effect.[10] Too often, however, markets have been slow to realize that

---

[9] Other studies reach similar conclusions but are less pessimistic about the prospects for Belgium and Ireland; see Giovannini and Spaventa (1991).

[10] Goldstein and Woglom (1991) examine the experience of state governments in the United States; Edwards (1986) examines the experience of developing countries. But Frenkel and

a government may have a solvency problem and have then reacted very sharply when made to face that possibility. This was true in 1982, when Mexico's debt crisis led banks to change their views abruptly about many other developing countries, and in the case of New York City a few years earlier.[11] Numerous reasons have been offered for this sort of behavior, from misunderstanding of the debtor's situation to the creditors' belief that some other party will bail them out.[12] Governments publish lots of numbers—more than most private debtors—but the numbers shed little light on the long-term fiscal outlook. The assessment of that outlook, moreover, requires a judgment about political prospects as well as economic prospects.

Why should the debt problems of individual EC governments be cause for collective concern by the Community or affect the monetary policy of the ECB? Buiter and Kletzer (1990) argue correctly that there is no justification for EC intervention unless those debt problems have large externalities, and they believe that the externalities are small. Hence, the national debt of each EC country can be expected to remain a national responsibility. And Article 104b of the Treaty, the "no bail out" clause, tries to make sure of that. It says that the Community "shall not be liable for or assume the commitments of central governments, regional, local or other public authorities, other bodies governed by public law, or public undertakings of any Member State," and that no member state shall be liable for or assume commitments made by the public entities of another member state.[13]

Two possibilities, however, led the authors of the Treaty to go further. The first is the possibility of political pressure from a heavily indebted government wanting the ECB to come to its aid. The second is the possibility of market pressure coming from the threat to financial stability posed by a prospective or actual default.

Economists are fond of putting the first possibility in Machiavellian terms. Heavily indebted governments, they say, will want the ECB to inflate away their debts by deviating from the maintenance of price

---

Goldstein (1991) point out that we have as yet no evidence that governments are sensitive to higher borrowing costs.

[11] See Begg et al. (1991), Goldstein and Woglom (1991), and Frenkel and Goldstein (1991).

[12] Kenen (1992) reviews the uncertainties surrounding the outlook for the developing countries on the eve of the 1982 debt crisis. Guttentag and Herring (1986) suggest that those countries' creditors suffered from disaster myopia—a systematic tendency to underestimate the probability of unusual calamities. Eaton, Gersovitz, and Stiglitz (1986) survey the large theoretical literature on relations between sovereign debtors and private creditors.

[13] An exception is made for obligations arising from joint projects. The clause does not cover the ECB directly, but it is more likely to acquire public-sector obligations as assets than take them over as liabilities.

stability.[14] Giovannini and Spaventa (1991) point out, however, that such governments would not gain very much, because some of their debt is indexed and much of it is short-term debt that would have to be rolled over at higher nominal interest rates if the inflation rate rose.[15] Begg at al. (1991) take a similar line, noting that this particular threat can be reduced by requiring the heavily indebted governments to index more of their debt before the beginning of Stage Three. The Machiavellian view, moreover, misrepresents the problem and is controverted by recent research. Highly indebted governments have not tried to inflate away their debts by adopting inflationary monetary policies; see Grilli, Masciandaro, and Tabellini (1991).

The pressure from governments is more likely to come when markets begin to realize that a government faces a solvency problem and refuse to roll over its debt without a large increase in interest rates. The ECB could not be asked to take up the debt directly, but it might be asked to make open-market purchases to hold down the interest cost of rolling over maturing debt. That is how the problem was posed right after the Second World War, when several central banks, including the Federal Reserve System and the Bank of England, held down the interest rates on government debt by open-market purchases, and the Banca d'Italia did the same thing in the early 1960s.

The second problem is related to this form of the first one. If an EC government were to default on its debt or were expected to default, holders of its debt would face capital losses, posing a threat to financial stability.[16] The ECB might have to intervene. It would not have to buy up the debt of the country facing default, but it might have to make other open-market purchases to stave off the threat to the banking system. The gravity of that threat, moreover, would not depend on the ownership of the debt at issue. The ECB could not ignore it even if the whole Italian debt were owned by Italian banks and other Italian investors. There will be a single banking system in Stage Three of EMU, and all of its parts will be linked via the ECB Funds market. In fact, localization of the problem might increase the threat to the banking system as a whole, because the potential losses would be concentrated on fewer banks and thus larger in relation to their capital.

---

[14] See, e.g., Froot and Rogoff (1991), who warn that national governments and central banks may conspire to increase their own inflation rates on the eve of Stage Three, undermining exchange-rate stability and forcing "one last realignment" of ERM currencies.

[15] Much of the Italian debt is short term, but most of it is not indexed. In 1989, the average maturity was 2.5 years in Italy, compared with 5.0 years in Germany and 9.4 years in the United Kingdom; see Begg et al. (1991).

[16] Giovannini and Spaventa (1991) say that the losses would not be large because of the short maturities, but that is not quite right. The prices of short-term bonds do not fall very much when interest rates rise, but maturity does not matter when a default is in prospect.

70

Economists who agree on little else seem able to agree that limits on budget deficits are not the best way to deal with the political dimension of the solvency problem. It would be better, they say, to make absolutely sure that the ECB will be independent and thus immune to political pressure.[17] Giovannini and Spaventa (1991) are almost alone in favoring limits on budget deficits to head off the solvency problem, because they are worried about market pressures stemming from the threat to financial stability.

Fiscal Hopes and Fears

There are two views of fiscal policy. Optimists continue to believe that fiscal policy can play a useful role in macroeconomic stabilization. Some optimists also believe that the governments of highly open economies can and should coordinate their fiscal policies. In this sense, the Delors Report (1989) was moderately optimistic. Although it called for limits on national budget deficits, it also called for policy coordination.

The fiscal provisions of the Treaty, however, reflect more pessimistic views about fiscal policy. Pessimists differ in the reasons for their views but unite in their belief that fiscal policy cannot do much good and may do much harm. Some say that budget deficits don't matter, because taxpayers know that deficits today must be offset by surpluses tomorrow to satisfy the solvency constraint, and they will reduce their spending today in anticipation of higher taxes tomorrow. Others concede that budget deficits matter but believe that democratic politics make it impossible for governments to use fiscal policy for short-run stabilization. Spending and tax changes are delayed by political bickering and take effect too late, so that they may actually amplify economic fluctuations. It is easier to win political support for measures that produce budget deficits than for those that cut them or turn them into surpluses.

The Treaty provides for policy coordination but emphasizes the need for surveillance over national policies rather than collective policy formation. Furthermore, the budgetary limits in the Treaty are aimed primarily at the solvency problem, not the stabilization and policy-mix problems. They are defined with reference to levels of indebtedness, not just budget deficits.

Policy Coordination in the Treaty

Under Article 103 of the Treaty, "Member States shall regard their economic policies as a matter of common concern and shall coordinate them within the Council" to achieve the Community's basic objectives. To this end:

---

[17] See Begg et al. (1991), Bovenberg, Kremers, and Masson (1991), Neumann (1991), van der Ploeg (1991b), and Wyplosz (1991). And Neumann would protect the ECB from market pressures too, by relieving it of responsibility for financial stability.

The Council shall, acting by a qualified majority…, formulate a draft for the broad guidelines of the economic policies of the Member States and of the Community, and shall report its findings to the European Council.

The European Council shall, acting on the basis of this report from the Council, discuss a conclusion on the broad guidelines of the economic policies of the Member States and of the Community.

On the basis of this conclusion, the Council shall, acting by qualified majority, adopt a recommendation setting out these broad guidelines.

The Council will report its recommendation to the European Parliament, but the Parliament will have no role in designing the guidelines—which is rather odd.

What will be done with the policy guidelines? Basing its work on reports from the Commission, the Council will monitor economic developments in each EC country and in the EC as a whole. If it finds that a country's policies are inconsistent with the guidelines or put at risk the functioning of EMU itself, the Council may make the "necessary recommendations" to the country concerned.

These provisions will not take effect until the Treaty is ratified, but the Council has begun to operate along broadly similar lines. Although it has not adopted explicit policy guidelines, it has asked each EC government to report on the policy measures it will take in order to achieve economic convergence and thus meet the criteria for entering Stage Three. These reports are being reviewed by the Monetary Committee, an advisory body comprising two participants from each EC country and two members of the Commission, which reports to the Council and the Commission.[18]

These arrangements, however, do not contemplate true coordination, which is usually characterized as a process of mutual adjustment causing significant modifications in the participants' policies.[19] Furthermore, a government cannot be penalized for failing to comply with a recommendation made under Article 103 (though the Council can publish its recommendation to put pressure on the government). But the Council *can* impose sanctions on a government that fails to eliminate an excessive budget deficit.

---

[18] The national participants serve as individuals, not as representatives of their countries' governments, and usually come from the ministry of finance or economics and the national central bank. The Monetary Committee has played a major role in designing realignments of EMS exchange rates. Under Article 109c of the Treaty, an Economic and Financial Committee will replace it in Stage Three, with a modified mandate and membership.

[19] See, e.g., Kenen (1989) or Dobson (1991) and the sources cited there.

Excessive Deficits in the Treaty

The Treaty sets out an elaborate procedure for identifying and dealing with excessive budget deficits. It is described here in detail because of its intrinsic importance and because a country that is found to have an excessive deficit will not meet the convergence criteria for entering Stage Three.

The Process

Article 104c of the Treaty begins with an outright declaration and goes on to define criteria for judging compliance with that declaration:

> Member States shall avoid excessive government deficits.

> The Commission shall monitor the development of the budgetary situation and of the stock of government debt in the Member States with a view to identifying gross errors. In particular it shall examine compliance with budgetary discipline on the basis of the following two criteria:

> (a) whether the ratio of the planned or actual government deficit to gross domestic product exceeds a reference value, unless

> — either the ratio has declined substantially and continuously and has reached a level that comes close to the reference value;

> — or, alternatively, the excess over the reference value is only exceptional and temporary and the deficit remains close to the reference value;

> (b) whether the ratio of government debt to gross domestic product exceeds a reference value, unless the ratio is sufficiently diminishing and approaching the reference value at a satisfactory pace....

> If a Member State does not fulfil the requirements under one or both of these criteria, the Commission shall prepare a report. The report ... shall also take into account whether the government deficit exceeds government investment expenditure and take into account all other relevant factors, including the medium term economic and budgetary position of the Member State.

> The Commission may also prepare a report if, notwithstanding the fulfilment of the requirements under the criteria, it is of the opinion that there is a risk of an excessive deficit in a Member State.

If the Commission concludes that a government is running or may run an excessive deficit, it will address its opinion to the Council, which will decide the question formally.[20] If it decides that there is an excessive

---

[20] At this stage in the process, the Council will act by qualified majority on a recommendation from the Commission and after considering any observations made by the government concerned. All subsequent steps in the process, however, including a decision to rescind an initial finding that a country has an excessive deficit, will be taken by a two-thirds majority of the weighted votes of member countries, excluding those of the country concerned.

deficit, the Council will make recommendations to the government concerned "with a view to bringing that situation to an end within a given period." If there is no effective follow-up, it may make its recommendations public. And if the government persists in failing to adopt the recommendations, the Council may "give notice to the Member State concerned to take, within a specified time limit, measures for the deficit reduction which is judged necessary by the Council in order to remedy the situation."[21]

All of these provisions apply from the start of Stage Two.[22] But more may be done in Stage Three. If a government does not respond to the final step described above, the Council may take one or more of these measures:

- require that the Member State concerned shall publish additional information, to be specified by the Council, before issuing bonds and securities;

- invite the European Investment Bank to reconsider its lending policy toward the Member State concerned;

- require that the Member State concerned makes a non-interest-bearing deposit of an appropriate size with the Community until the excessive deficit has ... been corrected;

- impose fines of an appropriate size.

And it can "intensify" these measures where appropriate.

The provisions of Article 104c are somewhat more flexible than those in earlier drafts of the Treaty. In the Netherlands Draft distributed six weeks before Maastricht, the reference value for the deficit was described as a "ceiling" and there were no "indents" beneath sub-paragraph (a), permitting the Council to allow for exceptional or temporary features or look at the trend in the deficit. But the reference values themselves are very strict. The one for the planned or actual deficit is 3 percent of GDP, the one for government debt is 60 percent of GDP, and the figures are to cover the consolidated deficits and debts of the central government, regional and local governments, and social security funds.

The Numbers

Before listing some of the problems posed by the criteria and reference values, let us ask what the Council might have done at the end of 1990 on the basis of actual budget deficits in 1990 and planned deficits for 1991 and the corresponding debt levels.[23] The relevant numbers for each EC country

---

21 This rather cumbersome phrasing distinguishes between the size of the reduction and the measures taken to achieve it. The Council's judgment will relate to the need for the reduction, not to the need for particular policy measures.

22 In Stage Two, however, the outright declaration at the beginning of Article 104c is replaced by the promise that member states will "endeavor" to avoid excessive deficits.

23 This exercise is meant merely to illustrate the ways in which the criteria might have been applied in 1990. It does not predict the ability of individual EC countries to meet the convergence criteria for entering Stage Three. That matter is discussed in the next chapter.

Table 1.
Deficits and Debts of the EC Countries as Percentages of GDP

Country	Entry	1986	1987	1988	1989	1990	1991[a]
Belgium	Deficit	-9.1	-7.1	-6.9	-6.7	**-5.7**	**-6.4**
	Debt	123.7	131.3	132.2	129.9	**127.3**	**129.4**
Denmark	Deficit	3.4	2.4	0.5	-0.5	-1.5	-1.7
	Debt	67.2	63.9	64.0	63.3	**66.4**	**66.7**
France	Deficit	-2.7	-1.9	-1.8	-1.2	-1.7	-1.5
	Debt	45.7	47.3	47.2	47.4	46.6	47.2
Germany[1]	Deficit	-1.3	-1.8	-2.1	0.2	-1.9	-3.2
	Debt	42.7	43.8	44.5	43.6	43.6	46.2
Greece	Deficit	-12.6	-12.2	-14.4	-18.3	**-20.4**	**-17.9**
	Debt	65.3	71.5	79.7	85.1	**93.7**	**96.4**
Ireland	Deficit	-11.2	-9.1	-5.2	-3.5	**-3.6**	**-4.1**
	Debt	115.7	118.5	115.4	104.7	**103.0**	**102.8**
Italy	Deficit	-11.7	-11.0	-10.9	-10.1	**-10.7**	**-9.9**
	Debt	88.5	92.9	96.1	98.9	**98.6**	**101.2**
Netherlands	Deficit	-6.0	-6.6	-5.2	-5.2	**-5.3**	**-4.4**
	Debt	71.7	75.3	77.4	77.6	**78.3**	**78.4**
Portugal	Deficit	-7.2	-6.8	-5.4	-3.4	**-5.8**	**-5.4**
	Debt	68.4	71.6	74.0	71.5	**68.2**	**64.7**
Spain	Deficit	-6.0	-3.2	3.3	-2.7	**-4.0**	**-3.9**
	Debt	48.5	48.7	44.5	45.2	44.5	45.6
UK	Deficit	-2.4	-1.3	1.1	1.3	-0.7	-1.9
	Debt	58.1	56.1	51.0	45.7	42.8	43.8

Source: EC Commission.

[1] Data for 1986-90 for West Germany; data for 1991 for unified Germany.

[a] Projections.

(except Luxembourg) are shown in Table 1, which gives actual figures for 1986 through 1990 and projections for 1991. (The projected deficits may differ from the "planned" deficits mentioned above and may also differ from the projections that would have been available at the end of 1990.) Numbers larger than the reference levels are shown in bold type in the 1990 and 1991 columns.

France and Britain would have met the fiscal criteria easily; Denmark and Germany would have come close enough. (Denmark's debt level was slightly above the reference level, but its deficit was small. Germany's "planned" deficit for 1991 was too big, but it would have been ascribed to "exceptional and temporary" circumstances in any 1990 assessment). And Spain might have been able to fend off an adverse finding by the Council. But six countries would have failed the criteria—Belgium, Greece, Ireland, Italy, and the Netherlands—because of big deficits, high debt levels, or both. (Ireland's deficit and debt level fell in earlier years, and its deficit was not very big in 1990, but its debt level was still very high.)

75

The Problems

Although the criteria are more flexible than those in early drafts of the EMU Treaty, they may still be too rigid, and the references values may be too tight. (1) A budget balanced at high levels of output and employment may move sharply into deficit during a recession—by more than enough to breach the 3 percent reference level. Such cyclical fluctuations are, of course, temporary, but the Council may not choose to interpret them that way, and governments may be forced to make procyclical adjustments in their fiscal policies. (2) It is impossible to be precise about the sustainability of a particular debt level, but the 60 percent reference level is far lower than one finds in the analytical literature on sustainability; see, e.g., Wyplosz (1991). It is indeed quite close to the average debt level for the twelve EC countries in 1990, so some countries had to be below it and others had to be above it.[24] (3) Including the deficits of regional and local governments will have wide-ranging implications. Consolidation may be needed for statistical standardization and to discourage manipulation of the data by transfers of revenues, expenditures, or obligations from one level of government to another. But it may also require some EC countries to overhaul their domestic arrangements substantially—for central governments to regulate the fiscal affairs of regional and local governments. The Protocol on the Excessive Deficit Procedure is explicit on this point:

> In order to ensure the effectiveness of the excessive deficit procedure, the governments of the Member States shall be responsible under this procedure for the deficits of general government.... [They] shall ensure that national procedures in the budgetary area enable them to meet their obligations in this area ...

The independence of the ECB may thus be guaranteed at the expense of fiscal subsidiarity within individual countries.

Some fear that EMU will not fly because its fiscal-policy provisions are too burdensome, but that judgment is too harsh. The limits on national budget deficits may inflict much pain on some EC countries, and that pain could be avoided by more fiscal flexibility at the EC level or, lacking that, more fiscal autonomy at the national level. Furthermore, some of the six countries that have large budget deficits, large stocks of debt, or both, will have trouble meeting the convergence criteria for entering Stage Three. More on that issue in the next chapter. Fortunately, some of the pain can still be avoided, because the reference levels for deficits and debts can be changed. The reference levels are contained in the protocol cited above, and the Treaty instructs the Council to replace the protocol with appropriate legislation. It requires unanimity in this particular case, but it does not prevent the Council from changing the reference levels.

---

[24] Nevertheless, the six countries listed above as having had excessive deficits in 1990 are the same countries cited by Corsetti and Roubini (1991) as being in danger of violating the solvency constraint.

V. The Transition to Monetary Union

There has been more debate—academic and official—about Stage Two of EMU than about Stage Three. The recommendations of the Delors Report (1989) concerning the mandate and organization of the ESCB were widely endorsed. But its recommendations concerning the transition to EMU were strongly criticized. Some critics questioned the need to require convergence before moving to Stage Three. Others questioned the wisdom of giving the ECB any role in the making of monetary policy during the transition to Stage Three.

The first two sections of this chapter look at those two issues and the debate about them. The remaining sections raise some questions about monetary and exchange-rate policies in Stage Two of EMU.

The Controversy Over Convergence

Chapter II described the processes and preconditions for entering Stage Three. In the process scheduled for 1996, convergence criteria will be used to determine whether it is "appropriate" to begin Stage Three and, if so, which countries are ready for it. If it is decided to defer Stage Three and nothing more is done until 1998, Stage Three will begin automatically in 1999, but the convergence criteria will still be used to decide which countries are ready. Nothing was said in Chapter II, however, about the convergence criteria themselves or, for that matter, the rationale for insisting on them.

The Case for Convergence
A number of economists wanted Stage Three to start without waiting for convergence. Dornbusch (1990), for example, argued that convergence has

already "peaked" within the core of the EC, and he urged the core countries, led by France and Germany, to move immediately to monetary union. A two-speed Europe, he maintained, would be better than a no-speed Europe, and there is the risk of that if Stage Three is delayed.[1] Others also wanted Stage Three to start before 1996 but for different reasons, and they denied the need to leave any country out. Stage Two will be hazardous, they said, and may be unecessary, as convergence will occur automatically in Stage Three.[2]

Stage Two *will* be hazardous—that cannot be questioned—and there may be accidents before it is over. There are four causes for concern.

First, governments may still try to pursue what Padoa-Schioppa (1988) called the "inconsistent quartet" of policy objectives—free trade and free capital movements, fixed exchange rates, and independent monetary policies. They have agreed to coordinate their policies, working through the European Monetary Institute (EMI), but that may be difficult in the next few years, for reasons given later in this chapter.

Second, Italy and other EC countries will have much trouble meeting the convergence criteria. They will face political and economic problems as they try to reduce their inflation rates and cut their budget deficits before Stage Three begins, even if it is delayed until 1999.

Third, a number of economists believe that the rigors and requirements of Stage Three may cause markets to predict that governments will use their independence before they have to give it up—that some of the highly indebted countries will opt for inflation and devaluation in a final effort to reduce their debt burdens—and that the markets' forecasts will produce exchange-rate crises.[3]

Finally, the next few years may be very turbulent—more so than the last few years. The EC countries will not be left alone to work off the effects of earlier shocks and policy mistakes. The world is not an economist's model, into which one can inject a single disturbance or policy change, then stand back to watch the economy move to a new steady state. Disturbances do not queue up like aircraft in a holding pattern, each waiting for the one before to clear the runway. They come in quick succession from many directions. Will the price of oil remain unchanged

---

[1] Swoboda (1991) took a similar position.

[2] See, e.g., Giovannini (1990), who advocated a quick "currency reform" by all of the EC countries and a rapid move to full-fledged monetary union.

[3] There are two variants of this argument. Some say that markets will expect the EC countries to undertake "one last realignment" before Stage Three begins, to offset cost and price disparities before the locking of exchange rates. This possibility cannot be precluded and will be discussed below. Others argue, somewhat inconsistently, that markets will expect the highly indebted countries to devalue unilaterally, even though that would bar them from entering Stage Three; see, e.g., Froot and Rogoff (1991) and Cukierman (1991). Both versions of the argument suggest, however, that the likelihood of an exchange-rate crisis is apt to rise as the deadline for entering Stage Three approaches.

in the 1990s? Was German reunification the last large shock from Central and Eastern Europe or perhaps the first of many?

Nevertheless, Stage Two may be necessary, because convergence may be necessary, and convergence will take time. Some sort of fiscal convergence may be needed to stave off the political and market pressures described in the previous chapter, and a closer convergence of inflation rates may likewise be needed to stave off political pressures.

A single monetary policy aimed at achieving price stability is expected to impose the same inflation rate on every ESCB country. But that will not happen instantaneously. Nor will it happen costlessly in the high-inflation countries, where output and employment may be heavily affected. The speed and cost of the adjustment will depend on the size of the change in private-sector behavior produced by moving to Stage Three.

If the Bundesbank could transfer credibility to the ECB by transferring responsibility to it, private-sector behavior might change dramatically, and one might then agree with those who say that the convergence of national inflation rates should be the outcome of Stage Three, not a precondition for starting it. An ECB with high credibility would find it easier to reduce inflation early in Stage Three than would national governments in Stage Two. It is harder, however, to transfer reputations than to transfer obligations. The ECB may have to earn its own credibility, and that may be very difficult without convergence in Stage Two.[4] If differences in national inflation rates persist until Stage Three begins, skepticism may persist, and the ECB will have to prove that it is truly independent and prepared to bear the blame for imposing the costs of fighting inflation—costs that will be very high if there is much skepticism.

The same point can be made without even mentioning credibility. It is a matter of responsibility. If the EC governments are truly committed to creating an ECB with the primary aim of maintaining price stability, they should start to reduce inflation before Stage Three begins. They should show themselves willing to impose the economic costs and bear the political risks of fighting inflation and thus prove their willingness to grant the ECB the independence it will need to maintain price stability. A decision to move quickly to Stage Three, without reducing inflation rates first, and thus to depend on the ECB to achieve price stability, not merely maintain it, would be an abdication of responsibility. It would force the ECB to bear the blame for the costs of reducing inflation—and make the ECB work harder. It would thus raise serious doubts about the commitments made at Maastricht.

---

4   Even with high credibility, moreover, the costs of fighting inflation can be very high. Dornbusch (1990) calculates "sacrifice ratios" for the EC countries. (The sacrifice ratio divides the change in the unemployment rate by the change in the inflation rate and thus measures the rise in unemployment that goes with reducing inflation by one percentage point). The ratios were higher for Germany and the Netherlands than for other EC countries whose central banks are thought to have less credibility. This result, however, may cast more doubt on the usefulness of the sacrifice ratio than on the validity of the conventional wisdom about credibility.

Defining Convergence

Some EC governments may have questioned the need for strict convergence criteria, and some had very real reasons to wonder whether they would be able to meet them. But they knew that Germany would require them, and EMU without Germany would be nonsensical. In the end, then, they agreed to four criteria, which are listed in Article 109j of the Treaty and explained in a protocol attached to the Treaty:[5]

- *Achieving a high degree of price stability,* which the protocol interprets to mean

    ...an average rate of inflation, observed over a period of one year before the examination, that does not exceed by more than $1\frac{1}{2}$ percentage points that of, at most, the three best performing Member States in terms of price stability. Inflation shall be measured by means of the consumer price index (CPI) on a comparable basis...

- *Achieving a sustainable financial position,* which the protocol interprets to mean that

    ...at the time of the examination the Member State is not the subject of a Council decision ... that an excessive deficit exists.

- *Maintaining the country's exchange rate within the normal EMS band,* which the protocol interprets to mean that

    ...the Member State has respected the normal [$2\frac{1}{4}$ percent] fluctuation margins...without severe tensions for at least the last two years before the examination. In particular, the Member State shall not have devalued its currency's bilateral central rate against any other Member State's currency on its own initiative for the same period.

- *Achieving a long-term interest rate indicative of durable convergence and of the country's participation in the EMS,* which the protocol interprets to mean that

    ...over a period of one year before the examination a Member State has an average nominal long-term interest rate that does not exceed by more than 2 percentage points that of, at most, the three best performing Member States in terms of price stability...

The Treaty goes on to say, however, that when the Commission and the EMI measure convergence, they should also examine current-account balances and the evolution of unit labor costs and other price indexes.

The first two criteria summarized above are related very clearly to the basic rationale for requiring convergence—the need to hand on to the ECB a sustainable situation and not make it bear the blame for imposing the

---

[5] The italicized passages paraphrase the provisions of Article 109j; the passages beneath them are quotations from the protocol. Under Article 104c of the Treaty, the Council must adopt legislation replacing the protocol on excessive budget deficits and may be free to modify its terms. The Council must also adopt legislation to replace the protocol on convergence but can only modify the "details" of the convergence criteria, which may leave less room for change.

costs of achieving one.[6] But the case for the exchange-rate criterion is weaker, and the interest-rate criterion may be redundant or misleading. What will be learned by asking countries to keep their exchange rates stable when the convergence exercise is aimed at asking whether a country is ready to enter a monetary union in which it will have no exchange rate of its own? If it has paid a high price to defend its currency, it should be praised for showing tenacity. If it has suffered in silence, moreover, without blaming other governments for its problems, it might be expected to respect the independence of the ECB and continue to be silent if the ECB's monetary policy caused it additional pain. But past performance on this score may be a poor predictor. Attitudes change. So do governments.

There is perhaps another rationale for the exchange-rate criterion— that the ability of the EC countries, taken as a group, to avoid exchange-rate realignments in the two-year run-up to Stage Three may measure their ability to bear the costs of adjusting to asymmetric shocks after realignments are ruled out by the locking of exchange rates. That sort of judgment will have to be made in 1996, when the Community must decide whether it is "appropriate" to start Stage Three. But the test should be applied to the EC as a whole, not to decide whether an individual country is ready for Stage Three.[7]

The inclusion of this criterion, however, may have a third purpose— to discourage realignments in Stage Two in order to confer credibility on the locking of exchange rates in Stage Three and thus protect the nascent monetary union from exchange-rate crises before it has moved to using the ECU as its single currency. Realignments in Stage Two might cast a shadow on Stage Three. If this is the reason for including it, however, the authors of the Treaty have not asked themselves how currency conversions will be carried out after exchange rates have been locked but before the advent of the ECU. There will be no need to use the foreign-exchange markets, and thus no need for intervention by the ECB or by the national central banks to defend the locked exchange rates. Currency conversions can and should be carried out through the ECB and the national central banks, in the manner illustrated in Chapter II. If the ECB and national central banks denominate their balance sheets in ECU at the beginning of Stage Three, start to think in terms of a single, consolidated balance sheet for the whole ESCB, and thus pay no attention whatsoever to transactions between its parts, there will be no reason for the ECB to worry about exchange-rate crises in Stage Three. Hence, concerns about Stage Three do

---

6 They may not be sufficient for this purpose, however, as sustainability may also require narrow differences in price and cost *levels*, not merely an equalization of the rates at which they change. This point will come up again in connection with the case for one more realignment.

7 It will be used in that broad way when, in 1996, the Community must decide whether to begin or postpone Stage Three. But it cannot serve that purpose in 1999, when Stage Three will start automatically. And it should not be used on either occasion to judge the readiness of any single country.

not really justify the use of an exchange-rate test to measure convergence.[8]

What can be learned from long-term interest rates? Unlike the other numbers used in the various convergence criteria, these are forward-looking numbers. They transmit information about expectations—but several sorts of expectations. If a country's long-term interest rate is high relative to those of other countries, markets may be forecasting an increase in the country's short-term interest rate or in its inflation rate or saying that there is a higher-than-average risk that the country will devalue its currency or default on its debt.

All of these are "bad things" from the standpoint of convergence. But most of them are covered by the other criteria. It may be reassuring for governments to know that the markets' views do not differ greatly from their own views—those that they have based on the convergence criteria. And when there is a difference between the two views, governments may want to reassess their own. The markets' views, however, may be badly biased. They will be affected by the markets' forecasts concerning the decisions that the governments are making. If markets come to believe that a particular country is going to be kept from entering Stage Three, they may forecast high inflation, devaluation, or default on the country's debt, and the country's long-term interest rate may rise. Conversely, if markets come to believe that a country is going to enter Stage Three, the country's long-term interest rate may fall. Governments should not rely very heavily on information that may be contaminated by the markets' forecasts of the governments' own intentions.

Measuring Convergence

How far are the various EC countries from meeting the four convergence criteria? It is hard to say much about the exchange-rate criterion, except to note that Spain and the United Kingdom must move to the narrow ERM band before mid-1994 if they are to keep their currencies within it during the two-year period prior to the date on which the Commission and EMI must start to prepare their reports for the Council.[9] Greece and Portugal, moreover, have not yet joined the ERM and must do so soon if they are to start with wide bands and move on to narrow bands before mid-1994. As for the rest, the debate at the end of 1991, after the large increase in German

---

[8] Begg et al. (1991) take a different view of the exchange-rate test. It is the *only* convergence criterion to which they would pay any attention, as they appear to believe that the success of the EC countries in avoiding realignments during the run-up to Stage Three is an adequate test of their ability to bear the costs of reducing inflation rates in Stage Three itself. They criticize the fiscal criterion because they believe that limits on budget deficits and stocks of debt are not necessary or sufficient to avoid debt crises. It would be better, they say, to insist that the highly indebted countries lodge their debts more firmly by lengthening maturities and to tighten prudential supervision by treating government securities as risky assets when measuring the capital adequacy of credit institutions. I have some sympathy for these suggestions and return to the first one below.

[9] Under Article 109j, the Council must render its decision on moving to Stage Three before the end of 1996.

Table 2.
Selected Economic Indicators for the EC Countries, 1990

Country	Inflation Rate	Interest Rate	Fiscal Deficit	Public Debt
Belgium	3.0	10.1	-5.7	127.3
Denmark	2.3	11.0	-1.5	66.4
France	2.7	9.9	-1.7	46.6
Germany	3.4	8.9	-1.9	43.6
Greece	18.2	n a	-20.4	93.7
Ireland	1.6	10.1	-3.6	103.0
Italy	7.5	13.4	-10.6	98.6
Netherlands	2.8	9.0	-5.3	78.5
Portugal	15.0	16.8	-5.8	68.2
Spain	7.3	14.7	-4.0	44.5
UK	8.4	11.1	-0.7	42.8

Source: EC Commission.
Inflation rates are based on GDP deflators, not CPIs (as required by the protocol); the latter would have to be standardized to offset cross-country differences in definition. Interest rates are yields on long-term government bonds. Fiscal deficits and public debts are percentages of GDP (and come from Table 1 in Chapter IV). The German data pertain to West Germany.

interest rates, suggests that the rest of the EC countries strongly oppose any realignment of EMS exchange rates, even one produced by revaluing the deutsche mark. They are not likely to devalue their currencies unilaterally and will thus keep them in their bands. Whether they can do so "without severe tensions" is another matter.

It is easier to say how far countries have to travel in order to meet the inflation-rate and interest-rate criteria. The relevant data for 1990 are shown in Table 2. The three best-performing countries in terms of inflation were Ireland, Denmark, and France; their inflation rates averaged 2.2 percent, and their long-term interest rates averaged 10.3 percent. This means that the inflation-rate cut-off would have been 3.7 percent in 1990, and the interest-rate cut-off would have been 12.3 percent.

At that point, then, there were five EC countries with long distances to go before meeting the inflation-rate criterion—Portugal, Greece, the United Kingdom, Italy, and Spain—but one of them (the UK) was making rapid progress. And four of those same countries had long distances to go before meeting the interest-rate criterion—Portugal, Greece, Italy, and Spain—though one of them (Spain) was likewise making rapid progress.[10] Using these two criteria together, three countries appear to be in grave danger of being kept from entering Stage Three—Portugal, Greece, and Italy.

---

[10] The table does not show a long-term interest rate for Greece, because it does not have a comparable rate. Its short-term rate is very high, however, suggesting that its long-term rate would greatly exceed the cut-off level.

It is harder to apply the fiscal criterion, because it is based on a process allowing for lots of discretion. But two countries—Greece and Italy—had blatantly "excessive" deficits in 1990, and their debt ratios were rising; they will have to cut their deficits sharply merely to stabilize their debt ratios.[11] Four more countries—Belgium, Ireland, the Netherlands, and Portugal—had large budget deficits and high debt ratios compared to the reference values in the excessive-deficit protocol, but they can probably make enough progress in the next few years to ward off excessive-deficit findings. Belgium and Ireland may not be able to cut their debt ratios down to the 60 percent reference level, but modest reductions in their deficits should cause decisive downward trends in their debt ratios, and they can also argue that their short-term debts are relatively small and do not pose serious debt-management problems.[12]

If forced to choose the EC countries least likely to be ready for Stage Three, even in 1999, one would have to pick Greece, Portugal, and Italy, which may fail two or more criteria. But problems could crop up elsewhere. Accidents may happen in Stage Two—and the longer it is, the more likely they are.

The Road Map in the Treaty

Once it was decided that the ECB would not begin to function in Stage Two—that the EMI would take its place—debate began in the IGC about the character and functions of that institution. As Italy and France were greatly concerned to maintain political momentum, they wanted the EMI to resemble the ECB as closely as possible. As Germany and the United

---

[11] A country with a balanced budget can expect its debt ratio to decline if it has a positive inflation rate or growth rate. If its debt is 80 percent of GDP, its inflation rate is 4 percent, and its real GDP is growing at 2 percent, its debt ratio will fall from 80 to 60 percent in five years. If it is running a budget deficit, however, its debt ratio will fall more slowly, and the ratio is bound to rise if the deficit is large. If the country described above were to run a budget deficit equal to 3 percent of GDP, its debt ratio would fall from 80 to 75 percent in five years, not to 60 percent. Countries such as Greece and Italy, then, are likely to experience increases in their debt ratios even if they start immediately to reduce their budget deficits. Countries such as Belgium, Ireland, and the Netherlands will begin to see their debt ratios fall after cutting their deficits modestly.

[12] The average maturity of Ireland's debt is 5.9 years, above the average for the EC as a whole, and the average maturity of Belgium's debt is 3.4 years, not far below the EC average; see Begg et al. (1991). Ireland and Belgium, moreover, have long-term interest rates well below the cut-off point for 1990, so they can probably lengthen their maturities without raising their interest rates above the cut-off point. A country such as Belgium or Ireland, which must worry more about its debt than its deficit, might ask the Council to render an opinion on the size of the reduction in its debt ratio and the increase, if any, in average maturity that would satisfy the Council. In fact, every country in danger of being found to have an excessive deficit might prepare a package of fiscal and debt-management measures and submit it to the Council. If the Council approved the package and the country proceeded to implement it fully, the Council might abstain from finding that the country had an excessive deficit, even if its deficit and debt remained above the reference levels after the beginning of Stage Two. A similar proposal was made by Giovannini and Spaventa (1991).

Kingdom wanted to maintain comprehensive national control over the conduct of monetary policy until it was transferred to the ECB, they sought to limit the mandate of the EMI.[13] The outcome was a compromise, but heavily weighted in favor of the Anglo-German view.

The IGC had to decide several other questions. What should be done to intensify policy coordination, particularly among the EC central banks? Should steps be taken in Stage Two to make the ECU-as-basket more attractive as an asset, to pave the way for the ECU-as-currency in Stage Three? Should the ERM band be narrowed in Stage Two, to pave the way for the locking of exchange rates in Stage Three?

What Will Happen in Stage Two

Stage Two will begin at the start of 1994, the EMI will be created, and a number of rules will take effect. There can be no "monetary financing" or "bailouts" of public entities (Articles 104 and 104b of the Treaty), and the excessive-deficit procedure (Article 104c) will start to operate, although sanctions cannot be imposed until Stage Three.[14] Finally, governments needing to grant independence to their own central banks must initiate the process in Stage Two (Article 109e).

The Structure and Functions of the EMI

The role of the EMI is described by Article 109f of the Treaty and by its own Statute, appended to the Treaty. It will be governed by a Council comprising a president, vice-president, and the governors of the twelve EC central banks. The president will be appointed for a 3-year term by "common accord" of the heads of state or government, on a recommendation from the EMI Council.[15] The vice-president will be one of the central bank governors and will be chosen by the EMI Council itself. The Committee of Central Bank Governors will be dissolved as soon as Stage Two begins, because the EMI will take over its duties.

Article 4 of the EMI Statute instructs the EMI to strengthen cooperation among the central banks and the coordination of their monetary policies, aimed at ensuring price stability; to hold consultations on issues falling within the central banks' competence and affecting the stability of financial

---

13 For more on this debate, see Crockett (1991a).

14 The surveillance of national policies under Article 103 will begin as soon as the Maastricht Agreement is ratified. The Council's role in making exchange-rate policy under Article 109 will not begin until Stage Three.

15 As the first president must be chosen before the EMI Council meets, the Committee of Central Bank Governors will make the recommendation. Unlike the president of the ECB, the president of the EMI can be reappointed. As in the case of the ECB, the president of the EC Council and a representative of the Commission may participate in the deliberations of the EMI Council but may not vote, and the EMI president may attend meetings of the EC Council when it is discussing matters relating to the work of the EMI. The EMI president may also appear before committees of the European Parliament.

institutions and markets; to monitor the functioning of the EMS and take over the tasks of the European Monetary Cooperation Fund (EMCF), which administers the EMS credit facilities; and to facilitate the use of the ECU and oversee the development and smooth functioning of the ECU clearing system. National monetary authorities are expected to consult the EMI before taking decisions about monetary policy. But the EMI has more to do:

> At the latest by 31 December 1996, the EMI shall specify the regulatory, organizational and logistical framework necessary for the ESCB to perform its tasks.... This framework shall be submitted by the Council of the EMI for decision to the ECB at the date of its establishment. [The] EMI shall in particular:
>
> — prepare the instruments and the procedures necessary for carrying out a single monetary policy in the third stage;
>
> — promote the harmonization, where necessary, of the rules and practices governing the collection, compilation and distribution of statistics in the areas within its field of competence;
>
> — prepare the rules for operations to be undertaken the national central banks in the framework of the ESCB;
>
> — promote the efficiency of cross-border payments;
>
> — supervise the technical preparation of ECU bank notes.

Under Article 15 of its Statute, moreover, the EMI may adopt guidelines for the national central banks on "the implementation of the conditions necessary for the ESCB to perform its functions" (but these will not be binding, as they have to be approved by the ECB).[16]

Finally, Article 6 of the EMI Statute allows the EMI to receive monetary reserves from the national central banks and issue ECUs against them in order to implement the EMS agreements. It may also hold and manage foreign-exchange reserves at the request of national central banks, but will do so as their agent and at their risk. (The French Finance Minister announced at Maastricht that France would place some of its reserves with the EMI.)

Article 8 of the EMI Statute declares that the central bank governors shall act "according to their own responsibilities" when participating in the work of the EMI Council and that the Council itself "may not seek or take any instructions from Community institution or bodies or Governments of Member States." These provisions echo Article 7 of the ESCB Statute.

---

[16] Unanimity will be required for the EMI Council to adopt the "framework" for the ESCB. It will also be required for decisions on certain financial matters and for decisions to publish opinions and recommendations concerning monetary policy. A two-thirds majority will be required to adopt an opinion or recommendation concerning monetary policy and the "guidelines" addressed to the national central banks. Otherwise, the EMI Council will use simple majority voting.

Chapter III examined some of the problems that the EMI will have to solve when designing the "framework" for the ESCB and "guidelines" for the national central banks. But something more must be said about the role of the EMI in coordinating monetary policies, the role of the ECU in Stage Two, and the outlook for the EMS.

Monetary Policies in Stage Two

The EMI will not make decisions about monetary policies, because the responsibility for those policies will remain in national hands. But it may "formulate opinions or recommendations on the overall orientation of monetary policy and exchange rate policy" and on national monetary policies and address them to the Council or to individual governments and central banks.[17] The EMI Statute, however, says nothing about the criteria that should be used to appraise the "overall orientation" of monetary policy or the policies of individual countries, apart from saying that coordination should be aimed at ensuring price stability.

The convergence criteria will be helpful, of course, in assessing and coordinating monetary policies. Countries with high inflation rates will have to reduce them. Furthermore, participation in the ERM will impose constraints on the setting of national interest rates. These requirements, however, will serve mainly to limit the freedom of individual countries to deviate from the general tenor of monetary policy in the EC as a whole. They do not provide a basis for setting or appraising the general tenor of policy.

For most of the last decade, of course, the problem has solved itself. The Bundesbank has pursued an independent monetary policy aimed at price stability, and the other ERM countries have pursued monetary policies aimed at maintaining a stable exchange rate vis-à-vis the deutsche mark. But recent events in Germany have made that arrangement less attractive. The arrangement was based on German fiscal policies and wage-setting practices that permitted the Bundesbank to control inflation without resorting to high interest rates. Therefore, it was comparatively easy for other countries to adapt to German monetary policy and even easier to justify that adaptation. But fiscal and wage pressures have mounted in Germany in the wake of reunification. They have pushed up the inflation rate and forced the Bundesbank to raise interest rates sharply. The situation could improve substantially in one or two years, but it has already raised questions about the viability of the old division of labor, and it may become necessary for EC central banks to make collective decisions about the "overall orientation" of monetary policy.

---

[17] Article 5 of the EMI Statute. An opinion or recommendation addressed to an individual government or central bank can be adopted over the opposition of that country's governor, because unanimity is not required.

How might this be done? One possibility was suggested by McKinnon (1982, 1984) in his plan for monetary coordination at the global level. Central banks might attempt to choose an appropriate path for an intermediate policy target—an average interest rate or monetary aggregate for the EC as a whole. Each central bank would then adopt a path for its own national counterpart of the target variable. They would not make identical decisions, as some countries have higher inflation rates than others, but the *sum* of their decisions would have to be consistent with the path chosen for the EC as a whole. Furthermore, individual countries might have to depart from their medium-term targets to deal with pressures in the foreign-exchange market.

McKinnon's own plan used a global monetary aggregate, and the national deviations were produced symmetrically and automatically by nonsterilized intervention on foreign-exchange markets. It was a gold standard without gold. McKinnon's rationale for his proposal was his finding that national inflation rates are influenced more strongly by the growth rate of the global money supply than by the growth rates of national money supplies, a phenomenon that he attributed to currency substitution, but other studies failed to confirm that finding.[18] The currencies of the ERM countries, however, may be closer substitutes than the currencies of the major industrial countries in which McKinnon was interested, and there is some reason to believe that the total money supply of the ERM countries exerts more influence on inflation rates in individual countries than do their national money supplies.[19] The EC central banks rely mainly on interest rates, not monetary aggregates, to influence aggregate demand, and they may find it more useful to base joint decision-making on an average interest rate rather than an EC monetary aggregate. But the subject needs more study.

The ECU in Stage Two

Anticipating the shift to the ECU in Stage Three, several proposals were made to enhance the attractiveness of the existing ECU and thus encourage its use. There were proposals to "harden" the ECU and to strengthen arrangements for settling interbank claims resulting from transfers of ECU-denominated balances. These issues, however, attracted too much attention. Why seek to encourage use of the present ECU when Stage Three will bring about a basic change in the nature of the ECU, from being a basket of national currencies to being a currency in its own right?

---

[18] See Spinelli (1983) and Goldstein and Haynes (1984j).

[19] See Bayoumi and Kenen (1992); this result is consistent with recent work by Kremers and Lane (1990) and by Monticelli and Strauss-Kahn (1991), who suggest that there is a stable demand function for the total money supply of the ERM countries.

Attempts to make the ECU more attractive would have been quite sensible if the EC had decided to pursue an evolutionary approach to monetary union of the sort proposed by the United Kingdom. The pace and success of the process would have depended crucially on the ability of the ECU to compete with the national currencies. Under the approach adopted at Maastricht, however, the attractiveness of the ECU used in Stage Two will not greatly affect the outcome in Stage Three, when the ECU-as-currency replaces the ECU-as-basket. Present arrangements for clearing and settling transactions in ECU will not have much importance in Stage Three, which must be concerned primarily with redenominating and improving the arrangements previously used to clear and settle transactions in national currencies, not with replacing them by the arrangements used for the ECU-as-basket.[20]

Care must be taken in Stage Two to guard against a breakdown of existing arrangements for clearing and settling ECU transactions. A breakdown could impair public confidence in the ECU and make it harder to move to the ECU-as-currency in Stage Three. No one can object, moreover, to the elimination of legal and other impediments to wider use of the ECU. More ambitious efforts, however, would waste time and energy.

Two proposals were advanced to harden the ECU in Stage Two. One sought to prevent any future exchange-rate realignment from reducing the value of the ECU basket in terms of the strongest EMS currency. This could be done by adjusting the currency composition of the basket after any realignment (i.e., increasing the number of units of the currencies being devalued to offset their depreciation in terms of the strong currencies, or even by increasing uniformly the number of units of every currency). Previously, by contrast, the composition of the basket was adjusted at five-year intervals in a manner that maintained its value in terms of each national currency but raised the shares of the currencies that had been devalued since the last adjustment. This technique exposed the ECU to gradual "softening" because it raised the amount by which another devaluation of those same currencies would reduce the value of the ECU in terms of the strong currencies.

The other proposal was to fix the composition of the ECU basket. This would not prevent a realignment from reducing the value of the ECU in terms of the strong currencies. In fact, it would preclude adjustments in the basket designed to achieve that result. But it would end the previous practice by which the quinquennial changes in the composition of the basket exposed the ECU to gradual softening on account of subsequent realignments.

---

[20] The present ECU clearing system, however, may provide the basis for constructing the transnational arrangements that will be needed to make same-day settlements between large banks in the ESCB countries. But changes might have to be made in the present system, and it might have to be lodged with the ECB, not with one or more of the national central banks.

The first proposal would have done more to harden the ECU, but at the expense of producing uncertainty about the timing of future changes in the basket; such a change would be required after every realignment. The second proposal, moreover, was seen to simplify contracts denominated in ECU, and it was widely endorsed by participants in the ECU markets. Hence, Article 109g of the Treaty fixes the currency composition of the ECU basket, and this provision will take effect as soon as the Treaty is ratified.

Exchange Rates in Stage Two

Recall the recommendations of the Delors Report (1989) about exchange rates in Stage Two. The ERM band would be narrowed, and realignments would be made only in exceptional circumstances.

The narrowing of the ERM band was seen as a step toward the locking of exchange rates at the start of Stage Three. It might have been useful as a way to prove progress and to capture in advance some of the benefits expected in Stage Three from eliminating the band completely. But the actual benefits would have been small—far less than proportional to the compression of the band—because a mere narrowing of the band would not have diminished the need for currency conversions or the fixed costs of making them.

Furthermore, a narrower band might have interfered with the targeting of monetary policies on price stability. Exchange-rate stability and price stability usually go together in the medium run. The currencies of countries with high inflation rates are likely to come under pressure in the foreign-exchange markets, forcing those countries to keep their interest rates higher than those of low-inflation countries. In the short run, however, the two objectives may come into conflict. The maintenance of exchange-rate stability within a narrow band can call for higher interest rates than those which a country might want to maintain with a view to reducing inflation over the longer term. Conversely, a country trying to reduce its inflation rate quickly may want to keep its interest rates higher than those of low-inflation countries.[21] By defining exchange-rate stability more ambitiously, narrowing of the ERM band might have raised the likelihood of those conflicts, and the recommendation was not adopted.

What does the Treaty say about exchange-rate realignments? It does not say anything about "exceptional circumstances" but does make realignments much less likely once Stage Two begins. A country that devalues unilaterally in the two years prior to mid-1996 will run afoul of the convergence criteria.

---

[21] Instances of this sort have arisen in the EMS; the case of the peseta is the most recent example.

There are nevertheless three windows of opportunity for exchange-rate changes—one wide open, one half shut, and one very narrow. Nothing in the Treaty can prevent a country from changing its exchange rate before Stage Two; nothing can prevent a country from *revaluing* its currency during Stage Two; and nothing can prevent a general realignment on the eve of Stage Three, before the permanent locking of exchange rates, if the realignment is agreed unanimously and designed in a way that does not affect the external value of the ECU.[22]

The case for "one last realignment" arises from concern that the final locking of exchange rates may leave some countries in unsustainable positions. These could be rectified thereafter only by enduring long periods of slow growth and high unemployment.[23] The size of the problem will depend on the time it takes for the EC countries to converge to a common inflation rate; the longer it takes, the larger may be the cumulative gaps between national price levels on the day when exchange rates are locked. The economic and social costs of dealing with the problem will depend in part on the degree to which the Community falls short of being an "optimum currency area" in the sense described by Chapter IV.

Four arguments have been made against another realignment. First, the experience of the Community suggests that changes in nominal exchange rates cannot change real exchange rates for long; the EC economies are too tightly linked by trade, and real wage rates are too rigid.[24] Second, the Community will resemble an optimum currency area at the beginning of Stage Three because the single market will have come into being, and the real costs of adjusting to an initial "misalignment" will be smaller than one might anticipate.[25] Third, a realignment just before Stage Three would undermine the credibility of the commitment to fix exchange rates irrevocably. Fourth, the expectation of a realignment would generate speculative pressures in Stage Two, which would make it very difficult for individual countries to satisfy the exchange-rate convergence criterion.

---

[22] See Article 109l of the Treaty.

[23] Article 109j of the Treaty appears to acknowledge this possibility, when it instructs the Commission and the EMI to take account of unit labor costs and other price indexes when assessing the degree of convergence, but it does not tell them how to interpret those numbers.

[24] Giovannini (1991) advances an odd variant of this argument. As the ECB will be expected to pursue a noninflationary monetary policy, the move to Stage Three will banish expectations of inflation, so that prices will become more flexible. With flexible prices, however, a change in nominal exchange rates will not change real exchange rates. This argument has some limited validity. If goods and labor markets are in equilibrium initially and prices are flexible, a change in nominal exchange rates will generate disequilibria, which will lead to offsetting changes in prices and wages, and there will be no lasting change in real exchange rates. But the case for a realignment is usually based on the supposition that goods and labor markets are not in equilibrium initially, because real exchange rates are misaligned. In that case, the credibility of the ECB's monetary policy, by diminishing real-wage rigidity, would allow changes in nominal exchange rates to produce lasting changes in real rates. (This point is repeated below in connection with the distinction between "active" and "reactive" use of the exchange rate.)

[25] That is the view taken by the Commission (1990).

No one can know whether there will be a significant misalignment of real exchange rates at the start of Stage Three, but one can say something more about the arguments against a realignment. When evaluating the first argument, that changes in nominal exchange rates are ineffective, it is important to distinguish between "active" use of the exchange rate to improve a country's competitive position and "reactive" use of the exchange rate to correct a previous deterioration. The distinction is very important in the European context, because some of the economists who have warned against using the exchange rate actively have nevertheless favored using it reactively. This may reflect incipient schizophrenia—but probably not. An active devaluation can create disequilibria in goods and labor markets, which are likely to intensify inflationary pressures and negate the impact of the devaluation. A reactive devaluation is much less risky when it is aimed at correcting a misalignment that is already resulting in disequilibria of the opposite sort—excess supply in the traded-goods sector and in the labor market—and that is the situation contemplated by those who believe that one last realignment may be needed.

Another distinction is needed to assess the second argument, about the contribution of the single market. The removal of barriers to factor movements is, of course, necessary to raise factor mobility and bring the EC closer to being an optimum currency area. As Chapter IV pointed out, however, the mere removal of barriers will not be sufficient, because other inertial forces will continue to operate. The narrowing of income differences and other disparities among the regions of the United States—a process driven partly by factor movements—has taken a very long time even in the absence of formal barriers to interregional factor mobility; see Barro and Sala-i-Martin (1991).

The third argument has already been answered. There is no real reason to worry about the effects of realignments on the credibility of the fixed exchange rates in Stage Three. Currency conversions will not take place in the foreign-exchange markets. They will take place at par on the books of the ESCB. The general public may be slow to understand this, but those who have the power to influence exchange rates by moving money around will quickly realize that the game is over.

The fourth argument, however, is hard to answer. If one last realignment is widely expected, it will be increasingly difficult to combat speculation in the run-up to Stage Three, and governments may find it impossible to meet the convergence criteria regarding exchange rates and interest rates. If they try to meet the exchange-rate criterion, they may violate the interest-rate criterion. One is tempted to suggest that the realignment take place earlier, before expectations build up, but that won't work. It will be impossible to guarantee the finality of any earlier realignment.[26]

Clearly, EC governments cannot rule out one last realignment but cannot talk about it either.

---

[26] Begg et al. (1991) tried to solve the problem by proposing a final realignment before the Maastricht Summit and the inclusion in the Treaty of a prohibition on any subsequent exchange-rate change. There are two problems with this solution. (1) The prohibition would not take effect until the Treaty was ratified. (2) The strength of the case for a realignment depends in part on the size and duration of future inflation-rate differences, and they are unknown now.

VI. EMU and the Rest of Us

Outsiders often complain that discussions of EMU do not pay enough attention to the impact of events and policies in the outside world on the economic environment in which EMU will operate and pay even less attention to the impact of EMU on other countries and the international monetary system.

The first omission is more serious for those who seek to understand how EMU will operate. The performance of the European economy will be affected by the exchange rates connecting the ECU with other currencies, and the policies of the ECB will influence exchange-rate behavior. The problem has been ignored completely by much of the academic literature, which has typically studied the effects of a monetary union in a two-country setting closed to the outside world. The problem was raised by the Delors Report (1989), which stressed the need for the Community as a whole to adopt an appropriate policy mix, and it was discussed in earlier chapters of this monograph, which criticized the fiscal provisions of the Treaty for not dealing adequately with that issue.

The second omission is easier to understand. Efforts to appraise the benefits and costs of EMU have concentrated on those benefits and costs which Europeans are most likely to experience, because Europeans will have to decide whether to move ahead with EMU and, if so, how rapidly. Should their national parliaments ratify the Treaty? Should Stage Three start in 1997 or be delayed until 1999? Nevertheless, EMU will have external benefits and costs that have to be appraised realistically.

Most economists agree that the ECU will become a major international currency, alongside the dollar and yen, once it has replaced the national currencies of the ESCB countries, but the consequences are not completely clear. Advocates of EMU sometimes argue that EMU will make the international monetary system more symmetric by reducing the role of the dollar and that this will relieve the United States of a heavy burden. Yet some of those who take this view once agreed with Charles de Gaulle that the global role of the dollar conferred an "exorbitant privilege" on the United States. Advocates of EMU also argue that it will facilitate policy coordination among the major industrial countries, because Europe will speak with one voice. Perhaps. But what will it say?

This chapter will examine these issues, starting with the implications of EMU for the rest of Europe, including EC countries that do not participate immediately in Stage Three, then turning to the implications for the monetary system as a whole. Like previous chapters, it will focus on the relevant provisions of the Treaty, not try to forecast the future of the Community or the evolution of the monetary system.

EMU and the Rest of Europe

Three groups of European countries must be considered here—those that will not participate in Stage Three immediately because they have failed to satisfy the convergence criteria, those that may join the Community before or shortly after the beginning of Stage Three, and those that will not join for many years thereafter or may not join at all.[1] The ESCB countries will be linked differently with each of these three groups.

The Links with Other EC Countries
Countries that do not participate immediately in Stage Three will be affected nonetheless by the policies of the ECB. How much influence will they have on its policies? Some EC governments, especially those that are worried about entering Stage Three immediately, wanted all of the national central bank governors to participate in the work of the Governing Council, even if they were not allowed to vote on decisions about monetary policy. Other governments wanted to exclude the nonparticipants from any formal role. A compromise was struck in the IGC, and it is reflected in Article 109l of the Treaty, which provides for the creation of a General Council as the third decision-making body of the ECB, and in Articles 44-47 of the ESCB Statute, which describe its role.

---

1 The countries likely to join the EC before Stage Three begins, mainly members of the European Free Trade Association (EFTA), may qualify more easily for immediate participation in Stage Three than some present EC members. (The EFTA countries are Austria, Finland, Iceland, Liechtenstein, Norway, Sweden, and Switzerland. They will be affiliated closely with the EC under the new treaty establishing a European Economic Area. Ratification has been held up, however, because the European Court of Justice has questioned provisions of the treaty relating to the Court's own jurisdiction.) Under the terms of the protocol allowing the United Kingdom to abstain from participating in Stage Three, that country's rights and obligations will resemble those of countries excluded from immediate participation (i.e., those with derogations). The latter will enter Stage Three automatically, however, whenever the Council decides that they are ready, whereas the United Kingdom can never be compelled to participate.

The president and vice-president of the ECB and all of the central bank governors will be voting members of the General Council, and the president will chair it. (The other members of the Executive Board may participate in its meetings but may not vote.) The General Council will "contribute" to the work of the ECB in various areas (e.g., collecting statistical information and setting personnel policies) but will have no role in making monetary policy. It will be "informed by the President of the ECB on decisions of the Governing Council" and can no doubt discuss them. But the ESCB Statute does not give it the right to be informed about matters *pending* before the Governing Council.

Nonparticipants do not have to transfer any foreign-exchange reserves to the ECB and are not subject to its jurisdiction. They "retain their powers in the field of monetary policy according to national law" (Article 43 of the ESCB Statute).[2] They *are* subject to the bans on monetary financing, bailouts of public entities, and excessive budget deficits, but they are not subject to sanctions for failing to correct excessive budget deficits.

What about policy coordination? What about the management of exchange rates between the ECU and the nonparticipants' currencies? The Treaty and ESCB Statute do not answer these questions. They say that the General Council will "take over those tasks of the EMI which...have still to be performed in the third stage" (Articles 44 and 47 of the ESCB Statute), and the tasks of the EMI include strengthening of central bank coordination and monitoring the EMS. But they do not say clearly that the General Council will inherit the *powers* of the EMI—the right to make recommendations to individual countries and to be consulted in advance about the future course of monetary policies.[3]

Furthermore, the General Council is poorly designed for coordinating monetary and exchange-rate policies. Suppose that Canada, Mexico, and the United States set up a committee for that purpose. Surely, the governors of the Bank of Canada and Banco de Mexico would expect to meet with the chairman of the Board of Governors of the Federal Reserve System, not sit with the presidents of the twelve Federal Reserve Banks and have the chairman of the Board of Governors preside at the opposite end of the table. If Canada and Mexico asked to join the Federal Reserve System, their governors would become the presidents of the thirteenth and fourteenth Federal Reserve Banks, but that is a different story.

---

2 But countries with derogations are required to make their national laws compatible with the Treaty and ESCB Statute and must appoint their central bank governors for terms not shorter than five years. The United Kingdom does not have to meet these requirements if it does not enter Stage Three.

3 Article 44 of the ESCB Statute, which transfers residual tasks from the EMI to the ECB was presumably designed to transfer the EMI's responsibilities for managing the EMS credit facilities. Furthermore, Articles 4 and 5 of the EMI Statute, which give the EMI the rights listed above, are drafted with reference to the "national" monetary authorities; they cannot be construed to give the General Council the right to make recommendations to the ECB.

The practical importance of these organizational matters will depend on the number and size of the countries that do not participate in Stage Three. If they are few and small, there will be little need for consultations about monetary and exchange-rate policies. The nonparticipants will have to adapt their policies to those of the ECB and peg their currencies to the ECU if they wish to qualify for eventual participation. If they are numerous and some of them are large, policy coordination may matter, not only to them but also to the ESCB countries. Questions remain, moreover, about the manner in which exchange rates should be pegged.[4]

The nonparticipants could peg their currencies unilaterally to the ECU and take responsibility for keeping their exchange rates within predetermined bands. They would use their own reserves for intervention and would set their own national interest rates at the levels required to maintain exchange-rate stability. They would probably intervene in ECU and thus hold some of their reserves with the ECB. If they were to assume these responsibilities, however, they might also insist on the right to change their exchange rates whenever they saw fit, without the consent of the ECB or the Community as a whole.

Alternatively, decisions and obligations could be shared between the ECB and the nonparticipants' central banks, under a residual version of the EMS in which the ECU would be one of the currencies involved, along with the nonparticipants' currencies. Central rates would be chosen collectively, the ECB would be obliged to intervene whenever the ECU reached the limit of its band, and it might also be expected to adjust its interest rates whenever that was needed for exchange-rate stability.[5] There would be short-term credit facilities like those of the EMS.

It may be objected that participation by the ECB in any residual EMS arrangement could impair its ability to pursue price stability. It was for this same reason that the IGC devoted a lot of attention to the roles of ECB and the EC Council in choosing exchange-rate arrangements vis-à-vis third currencies—a matter discussed later in this chapter. But unilateral pegging would have the same effect if the nonparticipants intervened in ECU and thus held reserves with the ECB; sales of ECU by a nonparticipant's central bank would increase the liquidity of credit institutions in the ESCB

---

[4] The Treaty is nearly silent on this matter. Article 109m calls on countries to treat their exchange rates as matters of common interest in Stage Two and to "take account of the experience acquired in the EMS. In Stage Three, moreover, these obligations will apply "by analogy" to countries with derogations. But the Treaty does not impose any reciprocal obligation on the ECB regarding exchange rates between the ECU and the nonparticipants' national currencies. Its silence can perhaps be read as an endorsement of unilateral pegging by the nonparticipants.

[5] It would still be possible for the nonparticipants to define the central rates for their currencies with reference to the ECU, just as they would with unilateral pegging, but the bands for the bilateral exchange rates between the nonparticipants' currencies would have be defined differently than the bands for the rates between the ECU and each of those currencies. Using the metaphor of the 1960s, the bands for the rates involving the ECU would form a "tunnel" and the bands for the other bilateral rates would form a "snake" and undulate within the tunnel.

countries, just like sales by the ECB itself under a cooperative currency arrangement.

Unilateral pegging, moreover, could burden the nonparticipants heavily. Consider a country that had failed to satisfy the exchange-rate criterion for participating in Stage Three. Should it be expected to do better on its own, without the benefit of the credibility conferred by collective arrangements, the obligation of the ECB to intervene, and large credit lines? And the case for cooperative arrangements is even stronger if several countries do not participate in Stage Three and some of them are large. Intervention could have bigger effects on the liquidity of credit institutions in the ESCB countries, and decisions about realignments could not be left to the nonparticipants acting unilaterally, as they could have large effects on the ESCB countries.

The Links with Other European Countries

As the terms and conditions for admitting new members to the Community are governed by separate agreements with those countries, the Treaty does not lay down the conditions under which they might participate in EMU. Some such countries might be ready to join it as soon as they joined the Community. Others might be asked to meet conditions equivalent to the present convergence criteria and might even be told to start trying to meet them before joining the Community.[6] The case for telling them to start in advance would be especially strong if, by the time they applied for EC membership, all of the EC countries were participating fully in the monetary union. New members would not be able to join an existing group of slow-speed countries, and there might be little tolerance for new slow-speed countries.

But EMU will have important implications for many European countries long before they apply to join EC, as well as for those that decide not to join or cannot expect to do so for decades. The EC will be the largest trading partner of most other European countries, including the independent states emerging from the old Soviet Union, and will look to London, Frankfurt, and Paris more than New York or Tokyo for short-term credit, long-term capital, and financial services. Hence, the ECU will become the most important foreign currency in Europe, and many observers expect an ECU zone to emerge in Central and Eastern Europe. It may indeed extend across the Mediterranean and into much of Africa.[7] Countries participating in this zone would borrow in ECU, hold most of their reserves in ECU, and peg their currencies to it.

---

6 The conditions would have to be equivalent, not identical, if there were no EMS in being and no successor to it, and it would make more sense to frame the inflation and interest-rate conditions in terms of average performance in the ESCB countries than in terms of performance by the three best-performing EC countries.

7 It could replace the CFA franc area and extend to other African countries having strong trading

Those who forecast these events invoke the history of the EMS, which came to resemble a deutsche mark zone as the central banks of other EMS countries sought to borrow credibility from the Bundesbank. Central banks in countries outside the EC may want to borrow credibility from the ECB, because of its commitment to price stability. They would then peg their currencies to the ECU and emulate the ECB's monetary policies.

It should be noted, however, that the one country in Central Europe that has followed such a strategy did not peg to the deutsche mark and might not have pegged to the ECU if that option had been open. Poland pegged the zloty to the dollar in 1990, partly because the dollar was used widely within Poland and was thus more familiar than the deutsche mark, and partly because pegging to the deutsche mark might have caused the zloty to appreciate against the dollar and make Polish exports less competitive in non-EC markets. When, indeed, the dollar appreciated early in 1991, the Polish authorities redefined the external value of the zloty in terms of a basket containing both dollars and deutsche marks in order to protect the value of the zloty from the effects of subsequent fluctuations in the DM-dollar exchange rate. Czechoslovakia and Hungary have likewise pegged their currencies to DM-dollar baskets. If these practices are indicative of events to come elsewhere in Central and Eastern Europe, ECU pegging may not happen quickly—although it will be increasingly attractive as the countries involved prepare to join the Community.

EMU and the International Monetary System

The completion of EMU will affect many countries outside Europe, and the ECU will become one of the world's principal currencies. It will assume and extend the roles that the deutsche mark, pound, and other EC currencies play today in the international monetary system. The completion of EMU will also affect economic and monetary relations among the principal industrial countries. These matters have been discussed extensively by the Commission (1990) and others,[8] and there is no need to repeat all of their findings. But some of their findings are questionable, especially those concerned with policy coordination in the Group of Seven (G-7).[9]

---

links to one or more EC countries. Its domain outside Europe, however, will probably depend on the evolution of pricing practices in major Commodity markets. If some of them shift from the dollar to the ECU, a possibility raised later in this chapter, many commodity-exporting countries may peg their currencies to the ECU and hold their reserves in ECU. (One cannot even rule out the pricing of oil in ECU rather than in dollars, which would extend the domain of the ECU into the Middle East.) Attempts are already being made to encourage the development of an ECU zone in Central and Eastern Europe; see, e.g., Association for the Monetary Union of Europe (1991).

[8] See, in particular, Alogoskoufis and Portes (1991). Some of the concerns expressed below are likewise expressed in that paper, and in Kenen (1991a) and Goodhart (1992b).

[9] The seven are Canada, France, Germany, Italy, Japan, the United Kingdom, and the United States.

The Global Role of the ECU

A national currency becomes an international currency when it is widely used by the residents of other countries. Governments use other countries' currencies to define the external values of their own national currencies and for intervening on foreign-exchange markets. They also hold foreign-currency reserves. National currencies are also used in international commodity markets for pricing and trading products such as oil; in foreign-exchange markets, where major savings of time and effort can be achieved by quoting the prices of many currencies in terms of a single "vehicle" currency; and in securities markets, where borrowers often issue bonds and other debt instruments in currencies other than their own. Furthermore, many firms and individuals hold foreign-currency balances for commercial and financial purposes.

A number of statistics are used to measure the roles played by national currencies in the international monetary system; they must be used cautiously but can provide interesting insights.[10] And most of them point in the same direction.

In the 1950s and 1960s, the dollar was the dominant currency in almost all domains—in the official and private sectors, in commodity and foreign-exchange markets, and in financial markets. The situation began to change in the 1970s, however, after the collapse of the Bretton Woods System and with the dismantling of exchange controls that had limited the usefulness of other currencies. The dollar remains the most important single currency and the dominant currency in some domains, but the deutsche mark and other Community currencies are widely used, along with the yen. The pace of change has been uneven. It has been rapid in those domains that permit incremental change; securities are issued in many currencies and in the basket ECU, and cross-border deposits are held in many currencies. It has been slower in those domains where savings of time and effort are made by using a single unit of account, as in commodity and foreign-exchange markets. Continued use of the dollar in these domains, moreover, has probably slowed diversification in other domains; if the dollar were no longer the vehicle currency in foreign-exchange markets, for example, governments would hold fewer dollars in their official reserves.[11]

---

10 It makes little sense, for example, to draw conclusions about the roles of the dollar, deutsche mark, and yen from the reserve-currency holdings of the major industrial countries. They have little freedom to optimize their holdings. The United States cannot hold dollars as reserve assets; it must hold marks or yen. And it cannot switch freely from one to the other without affecting the exchange rate between them. More generally, the currency holdings of the major countries reflect their previous interventions on the foreign-exchange markets. That is why the Commission (1990) uses the holdings of the developing countries to trace changes in the roles of the major reserve currencies—a practice suggested in Kenen (1983). One must also be careful to distinguish between changes in the quantities of currencies held and in their values; the latter can reflect exchange-rate changes.

11 The Commission (1990) stresses this difference between the two types of domains, citing Krugman (1984). The share of the dollar in the reserve holdings of EC countries has declined

101

How will EMU affect the situation? Consider the consequences of moving to the ECU in Stage Three. The immediate statistical effect will be odd. The share of the ECU in foreign-currency bank deposits and in official reserves will be much smaller than the sum of the shares of the national EC currencies on the day before the move. On the previous day, deutsche mark bank balances held by French, Italian, and other EC nationals would have been counted as foreign-currency deposits. When they are swapped for ECU, however, they will count as home-currency deposits, even though they are held at German banks rather than French or Italian banks. Similarly, holdings of deutsche marks by the Banque de France will be transformed into ECU and will no longer count as foreign-exchange reserves.[12]

There will be other statistical anomalies, and those who keep track of these matters will have to adjust their numbers and their thinking to keep from drawing silly conclusions. Once they have done that, however, they can start to look for the interesting effects—the degree to which asset holders will raise or reduce their holdings of ECU. There may be some substitution *out* of ECU by investors who have held several EC currencies to hedge against exchange-rate risk. They will have no reason to do that after exchange rates are locked—even before the ECU replaces the national currencies. There will also be some substitution *into* ECU, however, by EC residents and by others.

Most of those who have thought about this question believe that the shift into the ECU will exceed the shift out of it but that the net shift will be small, so that the gain to the EC will be correspondingly small. They have been conservative, however, and appropriately so, in assuming that the ECU will not replace the dollar in commodity and foreign-exchange markets. The rationale for using one vehicle currency in those markets tends to preserve the status quo—to prevent discontinuous switches from one money to another. But shifts to the ECU could occur eventually in some commodity markets, even in foreign-exchange markets, and would greatly raise the demand for ECU.[13]

---

sharply, because they have begun to use the deutsche mark when intervening to stabilize ERM exchange rates. They can do this because the deutsche mark is now traded directly against other EC currencies on European foreign-exchange markets; it is becoming a second vehicle currency.

[12] Alogoskoufis and Portes (1991) go astray at this point; they appear to believe that the ESCB countries will need ECU reserves and will thus switch from dollars to ECU. But the ESCB cannot hold ECU reserves, any more than the Bundesbank can hold deutsche mark reserves. The Commission (1990) argues that the ESCB will have surplus reserves because there will be no further need for intervention to stabilize ERM exchange rates. Accordingly, it says, the ESCB countries will be able to switch gradually from holding foreign currencies to holding real and financial assets that bear higher rates of return—although it will have to pay careful attention to the exchange-rate effect of the switch. The redenomination of deutsche mark reserves, however, and their reclassification as domestic assets will reduce the reserve holdings of the ESCB countries, and their remaining reserves may not be excessive.

[13] Alogoskoufis and Portes (1991) raise this possibility but do not cite the most compelling reason

Another institutional change will raise the relative importance of the ECU. When a single ECB Funds market develops in the Community, European banks will not make as much use of the Eurocurrency markets to lend or borrow short-term funds. In fact, the advent of an ECB Funds market may greatly reduce the importance of the Eurocurrency markets.

There is one more possibility, however, and it would cut the other way. The attractiveness of the ECU viewed from an external standpoint will derive in large part from its use in Stage Three by some of the world's largest financial markets—London, Frankfurt, and Paris. Its attractiveness would be reduced if the United Kingdom did not enter Stage Three. London will have large ECU markets in any case, but the survival of the pound as a separate currency would prevent the full-fledged unification of EC financial markets.

EMU and Policy Coordination

The case for policy coordination has been debated vigorously in recent years, ever since the revival of interest in coordination that followed the Plaza and Louvre Accords of 1985 and 1987.[14] This is not the place to review that debate, apart from noting that there is wide agreement on three points:

- Coordination among the G-7 countries has been sporadic.

- It has focused too narrowly on exchange-rate management and relied too heavily on official intervention in the foreign-exchange markets.

- There has been occasional coordination of monetary policies but little coordination of fiscal policies, despite repeated promises on that score.

The episodic nature of coordination and the emphasis on exchange-rate management are easily explained and may be inevitable. Governments take to policy coordination when they believe that something has gone wrong in the linkages among their economies, and changes in exchange rates or current-account balances are the most visible signs of trouble. They rarely engage in coordination to improve domestic conditions *per se*, although that is how economists tend to view the process and to evaluate the benefits and costs.

It is equally easy to understand why monetary policies have figured more prominently than fiscal policies despite the many promises to alter fiscal policies. Monetary policies are easier to change, and the power to

---

for it. They say that there will be more foreign exchange trading in the ECU than there was before in any national currency. True, but not the crucial point. It is the reduction in the *number* of currencies that may make the ECU a vehicle currency. With fewer currencies being traded, there will be fewer exchange rates and less need for the market to use a single vehicle currency.

14 Funabashi (1989) provides the most detailed discussion of the Plaza and Louvre Accords; Dobson (1991) provides a more general account of coordination in the G-7; Kenen (1989) reviews the academic literature, and some of the text below draws on that review.

change them is more centralized in most of the major industrial countries. In countries with independent central banks, however, internal coordination is needed to engage in international coordination and has not always been achieved. It is needed *ex ante* between each country's government and central bank, and it is needed *ex post* in the form of a commitment by the central bank to implement a policy bargain after the various governments have made one. Thus, Dobson (1991) argues that the difference between success and failure in the work of the G-7 has depended crucially on the degree of agreement between Bonn and Frankfurt.[15]

The Commission sweeps this problem aside in its discussion of policy coordination:

> For international policy coordination at [the] global level to become more efficient, it is of paramount importance that the definition of responsibilities ensures an efficient handling of [exchange rate] policy. The two major requirements for the Community in that respect are to be able to speak with one voice in exchange rate policy discussion at [the] G7 level, and to ensure consistency between its exchange rate and monetary policy objectives. In what follows, it is assumed that both conditions are fulfilled (Commission, 1990, p. 190).

Having solved this problem, the Commission goes on to argue that EMU will contribute importantly to global coordination. At present, it says, Europe appears as a collection of medium-sized policy centers facing the United States and Japan, so that the spill-over effects of decisions by individual European governments are small, while those of the United States are several times larger. The United States, it reminds us, is much bigger and less open than the typical European economy. Under this asymmetric arrangement, the United States has less to gain from coordination. It can even exploit the asymmetry by choosing its policies unilaterally without suffering much from similar behavior by Europe.

The Commission goes on to recite and dismiss the familiar arguments against a multipolar system—that it is unstable and leaderless. It concedes the need for leadership in any system but says that a multipolar system will produce better leadership than a hegemonic system. Alluding to the German role in the EMS, it says that:

> ... the leadership issue arises in any monetary regime, because the overall stance of monetary policy has to be set by a policy centre. However, this kind of *de facto* asymmetry within a formally symmetric system, which does not determine a priori which country should be the anchor of the system, is very different from the structural asymmetry of for example the Bretton Woods system whose rules gave the leadership to a particular country independently of the quality of its policy. Moreover, it can be considered desirable that the operation of the system rewards performance by linking effective leadership to reputation (Commission, 1990, p. 195).

---

[15] For a detailed account of the German experience, see Kennedy (1991).

It is hard to resist the temptation to quarrel with this reading of history. It is more important to point out, however, that the Commission's main argument can be turned around. If the United States is not particularly interested in policy coordination because its economy is large and relatively closed, will Europe behave much differently when it becomes a single economy, not much different in size and openness from the United States?

Alogoskoufis and Portes (1991) do not assume away the problem of internal coordination but pose it primarily as a problem of representation. Who will represent the Community in the G-7 when national finance ministers retain primary responsibility for fiscal policies, the Council has something to say about exchange-rate policy, and the ECB has the responsibility for monetary policy and for intervening on foreign-exchange markets? They also note that the Presidency cannot represent the Council in the G-7, as the Presidency rotates semi-annually, and the work of the G-7 requires continuity.[16] The basic problem at issue, however, pertains to internal coordination, and it cannot be assumed away. It resides in Article 109 of the Treaty, which reads in part:

> 1. ...the Council may, acting unanimously on a recommendation from the ECB or from the Commission, and after consulting the ECB in an endeavour to reach a consensus consistent with the objective of price stability, after consulting the European Parliament, in accordance with the procedure in paragraph 3 ... , conclude formal agreements on an exchange rate system for the ECU in relation to non-Community currencies. The Council may, acting by a qualified majority on a recommendation from the ECB or from the Commission, and after consulting the ECB in an endeavour to reach a consensus consistent with the objective of price stability, adopt, adjust or abandon the central rates of the ECU within the exchange rate system.

> 2. In the absence of an exchange rate system in relation to one or more non-Community currencies as referred to in paragraph 1, the Council may, acting by a qualified majority either on a recommendation from the Commission and after consulting the ECB, or on a recommendation from the ECB, formulate general orientations for exchange rate policy in relation to these currencies. These general orientations shall be without prejudice to the primary objective of the ESCB to maintain price stability....

> 3. ...where agreements concerning monetary or foreign exchange regime matters need to be negotiated by the Community with one or more States or international organizations, the Council ... shall decide the arrangements for the negotiation and for the conclusion of such agreements. These arrangements shall ensure that the Community expresses a single position. The Commission shall be fully associated in the negotiations.

> Agreements concluded in accordance with this paragraph shall be binding on the institutions of the Community, on the ECB and on Member States.

---

[16] They also raise some questions about relations between the Community and the International Monetary Fund.

This Article went through many drafts, and the language is cumbersome even now, partly because we have no agreed language for describing alternative exchange-rate arrangements. The term "regime" is not even used in Article IV of the Articles of Agreement of the International Monetary Fund, which speaks of the "monetary system" and the exchange-rate "arrangements" of members (and then refers to a "system of exchange arrangements").

The meaning of the first paragraph is fairly clear. It pertains to the procedure which must be followed before the Community will enter into binding arrangements like those of the Bretton Woods System, under which the external value of the ECU would be fixed by international agreement. The next paragraph is clear on certain points but not others. The Community will not adopt any less formal arrangement affecting the external value of the ECU unless the arrangement is fully compatible with price stability. But it does not say who shall judge that or how. Nor does it say how the Community will participate in international discussions, such as those of the G-7, concerning exchange-rate management.[17] In fact, this paragraph seems to contemplate "general orientations" adopted unilaterally by the Community rather than guidelines adopted collectively by the G-7, like those in the Plaza and Louvre Accords. The two are not mutually exclusive, as orientations adopted by the Community could embody arrangements developed by the G-7, but the path from the one to the other is not well marked.

There is one other reason for concern about the way in which EMU will affect the prospects for policy coordination and exchange-rate management among the major industrial countries. The ESCB will want to earn credibility by proving its ability to maintain price stability. It is thus apt to resist EC involvement in any form of exchange-rate management by the G-7 governments, especially if it involves large amounts of intervention on foreign-exchange markets. In the early years of Stage Three, then, the G-7 may find it harder to agree on policies and strategies affecting exchange rates, and EMU may lead to exchange-rate fluctuations larger than those experienced since the Louvre Accord. That would be ironic indeed, because EMU will grow out of the EMS, which grew in turn from the desire for a zone of monetary stability in Europe, yet the achievement of that goal may come at the expense of more exchange-rate instability in the world at large.

---

[17] The provisions of paragraph 3, on the conduct of negotiations about exchange-rate policy, are cited in paragraph 1 but not in paragraph 2.

A Concluding Note

How to sum up? By asking if EMU will succeed? Or even asking if EMU will happen? Those are the important questions, but no one can answer them. One can perhaps ask whether the blueprint for EMU makes sense, and the answer to that is quite clear. It does. The blueprint is imperfect and incomplete. Recall the many objections and questions raised by the Treaty and think about the work that has yet to be done to bring the ESCB into being. But think about the questions that had to be answered by the Committee of Central Bank Governors when it started to draft the Statute of the ESCB and by the Intergovernmental Conference when it drafted the Treaty itself. Most of them were answered sensibly, though compromise sometimes triumphed over clarity.

One more analogy between the United States and Europe may be appropriate here. The Federal Reserve System was likewise a compromise, balancing the needs of an emerging continental economy with regional interests and concerns, and it took many years for the new institution to solve the problems generated by the need for compromise. The imperatives of economic integration, however, produced solutions eventually, and the political system responded to the need for adaptation by changing the structure, mandate, and powers of the Federal Reserve System. That is bound to happen in Europe, and an adolescent ESCB will look very different from the newborn institution. But the speed of adaptation in Europe will depend critically on the further development of the Community as a political entity.

References

Alogoskoufis, G., and R. Portes (1991), "The International Costs and Benefits from EMU," in "The Economics of EMU," *European Economy*, Special Edition 1.

Angeloni, I., C. Cottarelli, and A. Levy (1991), "Cross-Border Deposits and Monetary Aggregates in the Transition to EMU," paper presented at the Milan Conference on Monetary Policy in Stage Two of EMU, processed.

Artis, M.J. (1991), "Monetary Policy in Stage Two of EMU: What Can We Learn from the 1980s?," paper presented at the Milan Conference on Monetary Policy in Stage Two of EMU, processed.

Artis, M.J., and D. Nachane (1989), "Wages and Prices in Europe: A Test of the German Leadership Thesis," CEPR Discussion Paper 296, London: Centre for Economic Policy Research.

Association for the Monetary Union of Europe (1991), "A Proposal to Create an Ecu Zone to Assist Eastern Europe's Transition to a Market Economy," Paris: Association for the Monetary Union of Europe.

Baer, G.D., and T. Padoa-Schioppa (1989), "The Werner Report Revisited," paper annexed to the Delors Report (1989).

Barro, R., and X. Sala-i-Martin (1991), "Convergence Across States and Regions," *Brookings Papers on Economic Activity* 1.

Batten, D.S., M.P. Blackwell, I.S. Kim, S.E. Nocera, and Y. Ozeki (1990), *The Conduct of Monetary Policy in the Major Industrial Countries*, Occasional Paper 70, Washington: International Monetary Fund.

Bayoumi, T., and B. Eichengreen (1992), "Shocking Aspects of European Monetary Unification," NBER Working Paper 3949, Cambridge: National Bureau of Economic Research.

Bayoumi, T., and P.B. Kenen (1992), "Using an EC-Wide Monetary Aggregate in Stage Two of EMU," London: Bank of England, processed.

Bayoumi, T., and P.R. Masson (1991), "Fiscal Flows in the United States and Canada: Lessons for Monetary Union in Europe," Washington: International Monetary Fund, processed.

Begg, D., F. Giavazzi, L. Spaventa, and C. Wyplosz (1991), "European Monetary Union—The Macro Issues," in *Monitoring European Integration: The Making of Monetary Union*, London: Centre for Economic Policy Research.

Bernanke, B.S., and A.S. Blinder (1992), "The Federal Funds Rate and the Channels of Monetary Transmission," *American Economic Review* 82.

Bernanke, B.S., and C.S. Lown (1991), "The Credit Crunch," *Brookings Papers on Economic Activity* 2.

Bovenberg, A.L., J.J.M. Kremers, and P.R. Masson (1991), "Economic and Monetary Union in Europe and Constraints on National Budgetary Policies," *IMF Staff Papers* 38.

Bryant, R.C., D.W. Henderson, G. Holtham, P. Hooper, and S. A. Symansky, eds. (1988), *Empirical Macroeconomics for Interdependent Economies*, Washington: The Brookings Institution.

Buiter, W.H., and K.M. Kletzer (1990), "Reflections on the Fiscal Implications of a Common Currency," CEPR Discussion Paper 418, London: Centre for Economic Policy Research.

Casella, A. (1990), "Participation in a Currency Union," NBER Working Paper 3220, Cambridge: National Bureau of Economic Research.

Chiappori, P.A., C. Mayer, D. Neven, and X. Vives (1991), "The Microeconomics of Monetary Union," in *Monitoring European Integration: The Making of Monetary Union*, London: Centre for Economic Policy Research.

Ciampi, C.A. (1989), "An Operational Framework for an Integrated Monetary Policy in Europe," paper annexed to the Delors Report (1989).

Cohen, D., and C. Wyplosz (1989), "The European Monetary Union: An Agnostic Evaluation," CEPR Discussion Paper 306, London: Centre for Economic Policy Research.

Collins, S.M. (1988), "Inflation and the European Monetary System," in Giavazzi, Micossi, and Miller, eds., *The European Monetary System*, Cambridge: Cambridge University Press.

Commission of the European Communities (1990), "One Market, One Money," *European Economy* 44.

Committee for the Study of Economic and Monetary Union (1989), *Report*, Luxembourg: Office for Official Publications of the European Communities [cited here as Delors Report (1989)].

Cooper, R.N. (1968), *The Economics of Interdependence*, New York: McGraw-Hill for the Council on Foreign Relations.

Corden, W.M. (1972), *Monetary Integration*, Essays in International Finance 93, Princeton: International Finance Section, Princeton University.

Corsetti, C., and N. Roubini (1991), "Fiscal Deficits, Public Debt and Government Solvency: Evidence from OECD Countries," NBER Working Paper 3658, Cambridge: National Bureau of Economic Research.

Crockett, A. (1991a), "The Role of Stage II," paper presented at the Estoril Conference on the Transition to Economic and Monetary Union in Europe, processed.

————— (1991b), "Monetary Integration in Europe," in Frenkel and Goldstein, eds., *International Financial Policy: Essays in Honor of Jacques J. Polak*, Washington: International Monetary Fund.

Cukierman, A. (1991), "Policy Outcomes in Stage Two and in the EMS Versus Outcomes in a Union," paper presented at the Milan Conference on Monetary Policy in Stage Two of EMU, processed.

De Grauwe, P. (1989a), "Is the European Monetary System a DM-Zone?," CEPR Discussion Paper 297, London: Centre for Economic Policy Research.

————— (1989b), "The Cost of Disinflation and the European Monetary System," CEPR Discussion Paper 326, London: Centre for Economic Policy Research.

De Grauwe, P., and W. Vanhaverbeke (1991), "Is Europe an Optimum Currency Area? Evidence from Regional Data," CEPR Discussion Paper 555, London: Centre for Economic Policy Research.

Delors, J. (1989), see Committee for the Study of Economic and Monetary Union.

Dobson, W. (1991), *Economic Policy Coordination: Requiem or Prologue?*, Policy Analysis in International Economics 30, Washington: Institute for International Economics.

Dornbusch, R. (1990), "Two-Track EMU, Now!," in Pohl et al., *Britain and EMU*, London: Centre for Economic Peformance.

Drazen, A. (1989), "Monetary Policy, Capital Controls and Seigniorage in an Open Economy," in de Cecco and Giovannini, eds., *A European Central Bank?*, Cambridge: Cambridge University Press.

Driffill, J. (1988), "The Stability and Sustainability of the European Monetary System with Perfect Capital Markets," in Giavazzi, Micossi, and Miller, eds., *The European Monetary System*, Cambridge: Cambridge University Press.

Eaton, J., M. Gersovitz, and J. Stiglitz (1986), "The Pure Theory of Country Risk," *European Economic Review*, 30.

Edwards, S. (1986), "The Pricing of Bonds and Bank Loans in International Markets: An Empirical Analysis of Developing Countries' Foreign Borrowing," *European Economic Review*, 30.

111

Eichengreen, B. (1990a), "One Money for Europe? Lessons from the U.S. Currency Union," *Economic Policy* 10.

———— (1990b), "Costs and Benefits of European Monetary Unification," CEPR Discussion Paper 453, London: Centre for Economic Policy Research.

———— (1991a), "Designing a Central Bank for Europe: A Cautionary Tale from the Early Years of the Federal Reserve System," paper presented at the Georgetown Conference on Establishing a Central Bank, processed.

———— (1991b), "Is Europe an Optimum Currency Area?," NBER Working Paper 3579, Cambridge: National Bureau of Economic Research.

———— (1992a), "Toward a European Central Bank," Berkeley, University of California, processed.

———— (1992b), "Labor Markets and European Monetary Unification," Berkeley, University of Caifornia, processed.

Folkerts-Landau, D. (1991), "Systemic Financial Risk in Payment Systems," in *Determinants and Systemic Consequences of International Capital Flows*, Occasional Paper 77, Washington: International Monetary Fund.

Folkerts-Landau, D., and P.M. Garber (1991), "The ECB: A Bank Or a Monetary Policy Rule," paper presented at the Georgetown Conference on Establishing a Central Bank, processed.

Frankel, J.A. (1988), *Obstacles to International Macroeconomic Policy Coordination*, Princeton Studies in International Finance 64, Princeton: International Finance Section, Princeton University.

Frenkel, J.A., and M. Goldstein (1991), "Monetary Policy in an Emerging European Economic and Monetary Union," *IMF Staff Papers* 38.

Froot, K.A., and K. Rogoff (1991), "The EMS, the EMU, and the Transition to a Common Currency," NBER Working Paper 3684, Cambridge: National Bureau of Economic Research.

Funabashi, Y. (1989), *Managing the Dollar from the Plaza to the Louvre*, Washington: Institute for International Economics.

Giavazzi, F., and A. Giovannini (1988), "The Role of the Exchange-Rate Regime in a Disinflation," in Giavazzi, Micossi, and Miller, eds., *The European Monetary System*, Cambridge: Cambridge University Press.

———— (1989), *Limiting Exchange Rate Flexibility*, Cambridge: MIT Press.

Giavazzi, F., and M. Pagano (1988), "The Advantage of Tying One's Hands: EMS Discipline and Central Bank Credibility," *European Economic Review* 32.

Giovannini, A. (1989), "National Tax Systems Versus the European Capital Market," *Economic Policy* 9.

———— (1990), "European Monetary Reform: Progress and Prospects," *Brookings Papers on Economic Activity* 2.

————— (1991), "The Currency Reform as the Last Stage of Economic and Monetary Union," CEPR Discussion Paper 591, London: Centre for Economic Policy Research.

Giovannini, A., and L. Spaventa (1991), "Fiscal Rules in the European Monetary Union: A No-Entry Clause," CEPR Discussion Paper 516, London: Centre for Economic Policy Research.

Goldstein, M., and S.E. Haynes (1984), "A Critical Appraisal of McKinnon's World Money Supply Hypothesis," *American Economic Review* 74.

Goldstein, M., and G. Woglom (1991), "Market-Based Fiscal Discipline in Monetary Unions," paper presented at the Georgetown Conference on Establishing a Central Bank, processed.

Goodhart, C.A.E. (1992a), "The ESCB After Maastricht," London: London School of Economics and Political Science, processed.

————— (1992b), "The External Dimensions of EMU," London: London School of Economics and Political Science, processed.

Greenaway, D., ed. (1990), "Policy Forum: Alternative Routes to European Monetary Unification," *Economic Journal* 100.

Grilli, V. (1989), "Seigniorage in Europe," in de Cecco and Giovannini, eds., *A European Central Bank?*, London: Cambridge University Press.

Grilli, V., D. Masciandaro, and G. Tabellini (1991), "Political and Monetary Institutions and Public Financial Policies in the Industrial Countries," *Economic Policy* 13.

Gros, D. (1991), "Reserve Requirements and EMU in Stage Two," paper presented at the Milan Conference on Monetary Policy in Stage Two of EMU, processed.

Gros, D., and N. Thygesen (1988), *The EMS: Achievements, Current Issues, and Directions for the Future*, Brussels: Centre for European Policy Studies.

Guttentag, J.M., and J.R. Herring (1986), *Disaster Myopia in International Banking*, Essays in International Finance 164, Princeton: International Finance Section, Princeton University.

H.M. Treasury (1989), *An Evolutionary Approach to Economic and Monetary Union*, London.

————— (1991), *Economic and Monetary Union—Beyond Stage I: Possible Treaty Provisions and Statute for a European Monetary Fund*, London.

Haldane, A.G. (1991), "The Exchange Rate Mechanism of the European Monetary System," *Bank of England Quarterly Bulletin* (February).

Ingram, J.C. (1959), "State and Regional Payments Mechanisms," *Quarterly Journal of Economics* 73.

————— (1973), *The Case for European Monetary Integration*, Essays in International Finance 98, Princeton: International Finance Section, Princeton University.

Kenen, P.B. (1969), "The Optimum Currency Area: An Eclectic View," in Mundell and Swoboda, eds., *Monetary Problems of the International Economy*, Chicago: University of Chicago Press.

————— (1983), *The Role of the Dollar as an International Currency*, Occasional Paper 13, New York: Group of Thirty.

————— (1988), "Reflections on the EMS Experience," in Giavazzi, Micossi, and Miller, eds., *The European Monetary System*, Cambridge: Cambridge University Press.

————— (1989), *Exchange Rates and Policy Coordination*, Ann Arbor: University of Michigan Press.

————— (1991a), *From EMS to EMU and Beyond*, The 1991 Bosman Lecture, Tilburg: Tilburg University Press.

————— (1991b), "Exchange Rate Arrangements, Seigniorage, and the Provision of Public Goods," in Frenkel and Goldstein, eds., *International Financial Policy: Essays in Honor of Jacques J. Polak*, Washington: International Monetary Fund.

————— (1992), "Third World Debt," in Newman et al., eds., *The New Palgrave Dictionary of Money and Finance*, London: Macmillan.

Kennedy, E. (1991), *The Bundesbank: Germany's Central Bank in the International Monetary System*, London: Royal Institute of International Affairs.

Kneeshaw, J.T., and P. Van de Bergh (1989), *Changes in Central Bank Money Market Operating Procedures in the 1980s*, BIS Economic Papers 23, Basle: Bank for International Settlements.

Kremers, J.M., and T.D. Lane (1990), "Economic and Monetary Integration and the Aggregate Demand for Money in the EMS," *IMF Staff Papers* 37.

Krugman, P. (1984), "The International Role of the Dollar: Theory and Prospect," in Bilson and Marston, eds., *Exchange Rate Theory and Practice*, Chicago: University of Chicago Press.

————— (1991), *Geography and Trade*, Cambridge: MIT Press.

Lamfalussy, A. (1989), "Macro-coordination of Fiscal Policies in an Economic and Monetary Union in Europe," paper annexed to the Delors Report (1989).

Masson, P., and J. Melitz (1990), "Fiscal Policy Independence in a European Monetary Union," CEPR Discussion Paper 414, London: Centre for Economic Policy Research.

Mastropasqua, C., S. Micossi, and R. Rinaldi (1988), "Intervention, Sterilization and Monetary Policy in European Monetary System Countries, 1979-87," in

Giavazzi, Micossi, and Miller, eds., *The European Monetary System*, Cambridge: Cambridge University Press.

McKinnon, R.I. (1982), "Currency Substitution and Instability in the World Dollar Standard," *American Economic Review* 72.

——— (1984), *An International Standard for Monetary Stabilization*, Policy Analyses in International Economics 8, Washington: Institute for International Economics.

Monticelli, C., and M.O. Strauss-Kahn (1991), "European Integration and the Demand for Broad Money," Basle: Economic Unit of the Committee of Governors of the EEC Central Banks, processed.

Mundell, R.A. (1961), "A Theory of Optimum Currency Areas," *American Economic Review* 51.

Neumann, M.J.M. (1991), "Central Bank Independence as a Prerequisite of Price Stability," in "The Economics of EMU," *European Economy*, Special Edition 1.

Padoa-Schioppa, T. (1988), "The European Monetary System: A Long-Term View," in Giavazzi, Micossi, and Miller, eds., *The European Monetary System*, Cambridge: Cambridge University Press.

Romer, C., and D. Romer (1990), "New Evidence on the Monetary Transmission Mechanism," *Brookings Papers on Economic Activity* 1.

Russo, M., and G. Tullio (1988), "Monetary Policy Coordination within the European Monetary System: Is There a Rule?," in Giavazzi, Micossi, and Miller, eds., *The European Monetary System*, Cambridge: Cambridge University Press.

Sala-i-Martin, X., and J. Sachs (1991), "Fiscal Federalism and Optimum Currency Areas: Evidence for Europe from the United States," NBER Working Paper 3855, Cambridge: National Bureau of Economic Research.

Spinelli, F. (1983), "Currency Substitution, Flexible Exchange Rates, and the Case for International Monetary Cooperation: Discussion of a Recent Proposal," *IMF Staff Papers* 30.

Swoboda, A.K. (1991), *The Road to European Monetary Union: Lessons from the Bretton Woods Regime*, The 1991 Per Jacobsson Lecture, Washington: The Per Jacobsson Foundation, International Monetary Fund.

Thygesen, N. (1989), "A European Central Banking System—Some Analytical and Operational Considerations," paper annexed to the Delors Report (1989).

Ungerer, H., O. Evans, T. Mayer, and P. Young (1986), *The European Monetary System: Recent Developments*, Occasional Paper 48, Washington: International Monetary Fund

Ungerer, H., J.J. Hauvonen, A. Lopez-Claros, and T. Mayer (1990), *The European Monetary System: Developments and Prospects*, Occasional Paper 73, Washington: International Monetary Fund.

van der Ploeg, F. (1991a), "Macroeconomic Policy Coordination Issues During the Various Phases of Economic and Monetary Integration in Europe," in "The Economics of EMU," *European Economy*, Special Edition 1.

————— (1991b), Budgetary Aspects of Economic and Monetary Integration in Europe," CEPR Discussion Paper 492, London: Centre for Economic Policy Research.

von Hagen, J. (1991), "Fiscal Arrangements in a Monetary Union: Evidence from the U.S.," Bloomington: Indiana University, processed.

Weber, A.A. (1991), "EMU and Asymmetries and Adjustment Problems in the EMS—Some Empirical Evidence" in "The Economics of EMU," *European Economy*, Special Edition 1.

Wyplosz, C. (1991), "Monetary Union and Fiscal Policy Discipline," in "The Economics of EMU," *European Economy*, Special Edition 1.

Group of Thirty Members

Mr. Paul Volcker
Chairman, The Group of Thirty
Chairman, James D. Wolfensohn Inc.

Dr. Pedro Aspe
Secretario de Hacienda y Credito Publico, Mexico

Mr. Geoffrey Bell
Executive Secretary, Group of Thirty
President, Geoffrey Bell & Company

Sir Roderick Carnegie
Hudson Conway Limited, Australia

Mr. Richard Debs
Advisory Director, Morgan Stanley

Sr. Guillermo de la Dehesa
Consejero Delegado, Banco Pastor

Professor Gerhard Fels
Director, Institut der Deutschen Wirtschaft

Dr. Jacob A. Frenkel
Governor, The Bank of Israel

Dr. Wilfried Guth
Member of the Supervisory Board, Deutsche Bank

Mr. Toyoo Gyohten
Advisor to the Board of Directors, The Bank of Tokyo

Mr. John Heimann
Treasurer, Group of Thirty
Chairman, Global Financial Institutions, Merrill Lynch

Mr. Erik Hoffmeyer
Chairman of the Board of Governors, Danmarks Nationalbank

Mr. Thomas S. Johnson
Former President, Manufacturers Hanover

Professor Peter B. Kenen
Director, International Finance Section, Department of Economics, Princeton University

Professor Paul Krugman
Professor of Economics, Massachusetts Institute of Technology

Mr. Yoh Kurosawa
President, The Industrial Bank of Japan

Mr. Anthony Loehnis
Vice Chairman, S. G. Warburg & Co., Ltd.

M. Jacques de Larosiere
Le Gouverneur, Banque de France

Mr. Stephen Marris
Senior Advisor, Institute for International Economics

Mr. Shijuro Ogata
Senior Advisor, Yamaichi Securities Co., Ltd.

Dr. Sylvia Ostry
Chairman, Center for International Studies, The University of Toronto

Dr. Tommaso Padoa-Schioppa
Deputy Director General, Banca d'Italia

Mr. Karl Otto Pöhl
Partner, Sal Oppenheim Jr. & Cie. KGaA

Mr. William Rhodes
Vice Chairman, Citibank

Mr. Robert V. Roosa
Partner, Brown Brothers Harriman & Co.

Mr. Anthony M. Solomon
Chairman, Economics Transition Program, Institute for East West Security

M. Jean-Claude Trichet
Directeur du Trésor, France

Mr. Rodney B. Wagner
Vice-Chairman, Credit Policy Committee, J. P. Morgan & Co.

Dr. Marina v N. Whitman
Vice-President & Group Executive, General Motors Corporation

Rt. Hon. Lord Richardson of Duntisbourne KG
Honorary Chairman, Group of Thirty

Group of Thirty Publications since 1985

Reports:

The Foreign Exchange Market in the 1980s
The Foreign Exchange Market Study Group. 1985

Countertrade in the World Economy
Robert V. Roosa, et al. 1985

Outlook for Mineral Commodities
R. H. Carnegie. 1986

Inflation Stabilization with Incomes Policy Support
Rudiger Dornbusch and Mario Henrique Simonsen, with discussion by Mario Brodersohn, Michael Bruno, G. G. Johnson. 1987

Finance for Developing Countries
Richard A. Debs, David L. Roberts, Eli M. Remolona. 1987

International Macroeconomic Policy Co-ordination
Policy Co-ordination Study Group. 1988

Perestroika: A Sustainable Process for Change
John P. Hardt and Sheila N. Heslin, with commentary by Oleg Bogomolov. 1989

The Risks Facing the World Economy
The Risks Facing the World Economy Study Group. 1991

Financing Eastern Europe
Richard A. Debs, Harvey Shapiro and Charles Taylor. 1991

The Summit Process and Collective Security: Future

Responsibility Sharing
The Summit Reform Study Group. 1991

Sea Changes in Latin America
Pedro Aspe, Andres Bianchi and Domingo Cavallo, with discussion by S.T. Beza and William Rhodes. 1992

Special Reports:
Clearance and Settlement Systems in the World's Securities Markets
Steering & Working Committees of the Securities Clearance and Settlement Study. 1988

Clearance and Settlement Systems: Status Reports, Spring 1990
Various Authors. 1990

Conference on Clearance and Settlement Systems; London, March 1990: Speeches
Various Authors. 1990

Clearance and Settlement Systems: Status Reports, Year-End 1990
Various Authors. 1991

Occasional Papers:
16. **Policy Lessons of the Development Experience**
Helen Hughes. 1985

17. **Japan's Role in the Emerging Global Securities Markets**
Hamish McRae. 1985

18. **Japan as Capital Exporter and the World Economy**
Masaru Yoshitomi. 1985

19. **The Dollar's Borrowed Strength**
Otmar Emminger. 1985

20. **The ECU: Birth of a New Currency**
Polly Reynolds Allen. 1986

21. **The United States and Japan in the International Monetary System 1946-1985**
Robert V. Roosa. 1986

22. **The Japanese Trade Surplus and Capital Outflow**
Michiya Matsukawa. 1987